Contents

Contents

Name _____

Animal Habitats

Draw a picture of an animal on this page. Then answer the questions.

```



```

1. What do you think this animal needs in order to live?

_____

_____

2. In what kinds of places do you think this animal could live?

_____

_____

3. What do you like best about this animal? Why?

_____

_____

Name _____

Animal Habitats

As you read each selection in Animal Habitats, fill in the boxes of the chart that apply to the selection.

	How do the people and animals meet?	What happens when the people and animals meet?
Nights of the Pufflings		
Seal Surfer		
Two Days in May		

Name _____

Bird Words

Write the correct word next to each definition. Then find and circle all seven words in the word search.

1. Holes animals use as underground nests.

   _____

2. To do something risky. _____

3. Sending upwards like a rocket. _____

4. On or to the shore. _____

5. Acting on a feeling, without thinking. _____

6. Having no people living there. _____

7. Stuck or trapped. _____

Vocabulary
ashore
burrows
instinctively
launching
stranded
uninhabited
venture

```
I N S T I N C T I V E L Y
W P U N I N H A B I T E D
G N L N R T O N Q M R G L
W V A L P V E N T U R E A
K P A S H O R E W O T J U
B B P H A X D E J L I Y N
E K U S A J U X V B M R C
C W K R B N B S W G S U H
C V S T R A N D E D R D I
R O J A X O Q T S G K C N
Q W M M O D W R Q I C A G
I N S A F P A S Y C R C B
```

Name _____

Puffin Fact Chart

Why Puffins Come to the Island (page 21)	**What Growing Puffin Chicks Do (page 25)**
1. _____ _____ 2. _____ _____	1. _____ _____ 2. _____ _____ 3. _____ _____
What Puffins Look Like and What They Do (pages 22–23)	**What Happens on Pufflings' First Flight to the Sea (pages 28–32)**
1. _____ _____ 2. _____ _____ 3. _____ _____ 4. _____ _____	1. _____ _____ 2. _____ _____ 3. _____ _____ 4. _____ _____

Name _____

The Problem with Pufflings

Finish each sentence about *Nights of the Pufflings*.

1. After a winter at sea, puffins return to Halla's island because

    _____

2. Halla and her friends can't see the baby chicks because

    _____

3. In August, the young pufflings come out of their burrows because

    _____

4. Pufflings that don't make it to the ocean are in danger because

    _____

5. The children wander through the streets at night because

    _____

6. The next day the children take their cardboard boxes to the beach because

    _____

Name _____

Fact or Opinion?

Read the story. Then go on to the next page.

A Bird by Any Other Name

Another name for a pigeon is a rock dove, and, indeed, pigeons belong to the same bird family as doves. Doves are thought to be clean, pretty, and gentle. But pigeons really look very dirty. They can be messy too!

If you live in a city, you've probably seen lots of them in parks and other places where people eat their lunch. To find food, pigeons will make pests of themselves. In some cities the return of falcons and hawks has cut down on pigeon numbers. Be glad that there are fewer pigeons around!

Some people train pigeons to fly home from many miles away. These pigeons are known as homing pigeons. They can carry messages. Scientists think that sunlight and Earth's magnetism help the pigeons know where to fly.

In the early 1800s, millions of passenger pigeons lived in North America. As settlers moved west, they hunted the birds for meat, fat, and feathers. By 1880, most passenger pigeons were gone. The last one died in a zoo in 1914. It's sad to think there are no more passenger pigeons.

Name _____

Fact or Opinion? continued

**Read each statement below. Decide if it is a fact or opinion.
Write *fact* or *opinion* on the line.**

1. Another name for a pigeon is a rock dove. _____

2. Pigeons belong to the same family of birds as doves. _____

3. Pigeons are really very dirty birds. _____

4. You can see pigeons in parks. _____

5. Pigeons make pests of themselves. _____

6. You should be glad that there are fewer pigeons around. _____

7. Homing pigeons can carry messages. _____

8. The last passenger pigeon died in 1914. _____

9. It's sad that there are no more passenger pigeons. _____

How did you figure out which of the statements above were opinions?
Write a sentence to explain your thinking.

_____

_____

Name _____

Dictionary Disaster

The writers of this dictionary page need your help. They have included each word, its part of speech, and its definition. Now finish each entry by dividing the word into syllables.

Example: notebook *noun* A book with blank pages to write on.

note • book

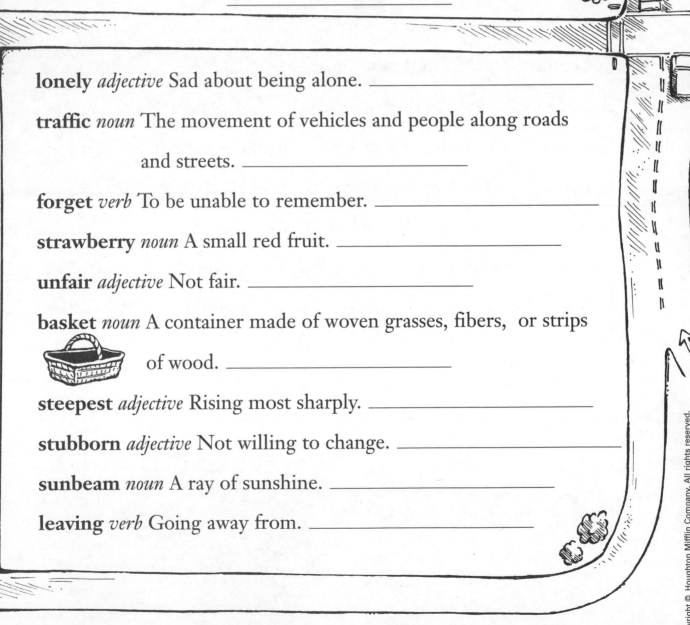

lonely *adjective* Sad about being alone. _____

traffic *noun* The movement of vehicles and people along roads

and streets. _____

forget *verb* To be unable to remember. _____

strawberry *noun* A small red fruit. _____

unfair *adjective* Not fair. _____

basket *noun* A container made of woven grasses, fibers, or strips

of wood. _____

steepest *adjective* Rising most sharply. _____

stubborn *adjective* Not willing to change. _____

sunbeam *noun* A ray of sunshine. _____

leaving *verb* Going away from. _____

Name _____

The Vowel + /r/ Sounds in *hair*

There are three different ways to spell the /âr/ sounds heard in *hair*. The three patterns are as follows:

are, as in c**are**

air, as in h**air**

ear, as in b**ear**

▶ In the starred word *where*, the /âr/ sounds are spelled *ere*.

Write each Spelling Word under its spelling of the /âr/ sounds.

Spelling Words

1. hair
2. care
3. chair
4. pair
5. bear
6. where*
7. scare
8. air
9. pear
10. bare
11. fair
12. share

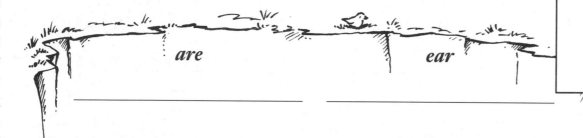

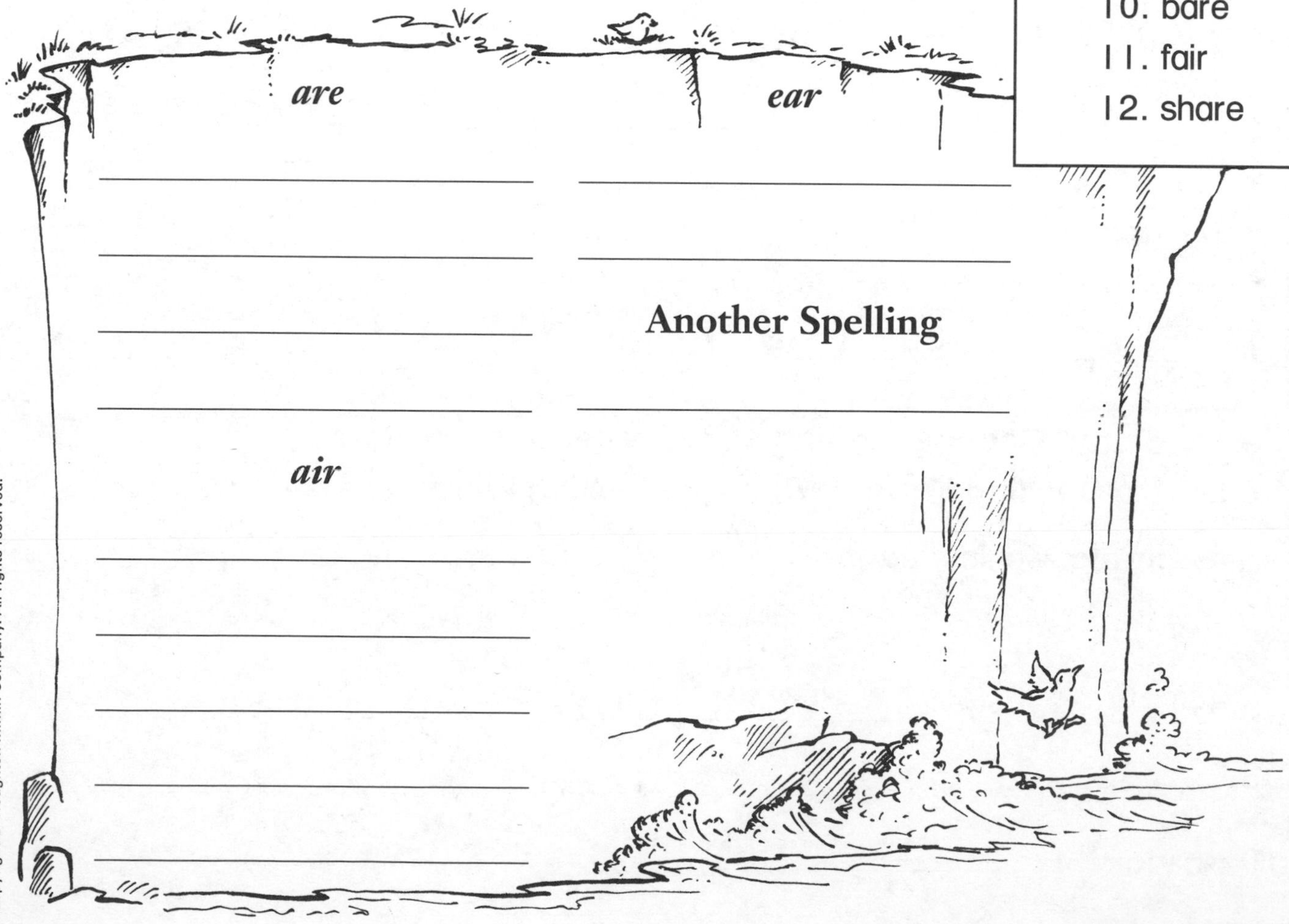

are

ear

Another Spelling

air

Spelling Spree

Hink Pinks Write the Spelling Word that fits the clue
and rhymes with the given word.

Example: a purchase during an **sky** __buy__
airplane flight

1. a long look by a large, furry animal _____ **stare**
2. a rip in a seat cushion _____ **tear**
3. a hairless rabbit _____ **hare**
4. taking care of a female horse **mare** _____
5. products made from animal fur _____ **ware**
6. a challenge to eat a fruit _____ **dare**
7. a frightening-looking costume _____ **wear**

Spelling Words

1. hair
2. care
3. chair
4. pair
5. bear
6. where*
7. scare
8. air
9. pear
10. bare
11. fair
12. share

1. _____ 5. _____

2. _____ 6. _____

3. _____ 7. _____

4. _____

Letter Swap Change the underlined letter in each word
to make a Spelling Word. Write the Spelling Word.

Example: would *could*

8. fai_l_ _____ 11. _f_ir _____

9. _t_here _____ 12. pai_d_ _____

10. sha_p_e _____

Name _____

Proofreading and Writing

Proofreading Circle the five misspelled Spelling
Words. Then write each word correctly.

Iceland at a Glance

Iceland is an island in the Atlantic Ocean. Most
visitors arrive by aer. Few travel to the center of the
island, whare glaciers cover most of the land. Even
the coastal areas are almost bair of trees. The people
of Iceland take kare to make visitors feel welcome.
They are happy to shear their favorite foods with
you. If you go to this unusual island, you'll enjoy
your visit!

Spelling Words

1. hair
2. care
3. chair
4. pair
5. bear
6. where*
7. scare
8. air
9. pear
10. bare
11. fair
12. share

1. _____   4. _____

2. _____   5. _____

3. _____

Write a Notice The children of Heimaey Island do their best
to rescue the lost pufflings. You want to help by writing a notice
warning people to watch out for the young birds. How would
you get people's attention? What would you ask them to do?

**On a separate sheet of paper, write a notice to the people of
Heimaey Island. Use Spelling Words from the list.**

Name _____

Name the Part of Speech

Read each sentence. Decide the part of speech for each underlined word. Then choose the correct meaning. Write the correct letter in the blank.

1. Halla <u>spots</u> her first puffin of the season. _____
   a. *noun* Small marks or stains.
   b. *verb* Finds or locates.

2. The puffins <u>land</u> while the children are in school. _____
   a. *noun* The part of Earth not covered by water.
   b. *verb* To come down on a surface.

3. Many puffins ride the <u>waves</u> that are close to shore. _____
   a. *noun* Ridges or swells moving across a body of water.
   b. *verb* Flaps or flutters.

4. Halla's friend <u>spies</u> a puffin overhead. _____
   a. *noun* Secret agents who get information about an enemy.
   b. *verb* Catches sight of; sees.

5. The pufflings cannot take off from flat <u>ground</u>. _____
   a. *noun* The solid surface of the earth; land.
   b. *verb* To cause to touch the bottom of a body of water.

6. Halla wishes the little birds a safe <u>journey</u>. _____
   a. *noun* A trip; a passage from one place to another.
   b. *verb* To make a journey.

Name _____

Completing with *be*

Complete each sentence. Fill in the blank with the form of *be* that matches the subject. Use the tense named in parentheses.

1. The story _____ about pufflings. (present)

2. We _____ curious about these birds. (present)

3. The pufflings _____ beautiful. (past)

4. Halla _____ ready. (past)

5. She _____ very clever. (present)

6. The birds _____ confused by the village lights. (present)

7. Children _____ everywhere, searching for lost birds. (past)

8. One small puffling _____ stranded in the village. (past)

9. The students _____ very brave. (past)

10. I _____ glad they rescued the pufflings. (present)

Name _____

Be-ing Smart

The Irregular Verb *be*		
Subject	**Present**	**Past**
I	am	was
you	are	were
he, she, it, singular noun	is	was
we, they	are	were
plural noun	are	were

**Use the verbs in the chart to complete these sentences.
Cross off each verb in the chart when you use it.**

1. The puffin _____ a beautiful bird. (am, is)

2. I _____ sorry that some get stranded. (am, are)

3. You _____ very helpful during the rescue. (was, were)

4. The students _____ heroes. (are, am)

5. We _____ surprised by the number of pufflings. (was, were)

6. I _____ almost frightened by the strange noises. (was, were)

7. The puffling's cry _____ sad. (were, was)

8. The young birds _____ hungry. (was, were)

9. You _____ curious about pufflings. (is, are)

10. They _____ fascinating animals. (are, is)

Name _____

Forms of the Verb *be*

Good writers are careful to use the correct form of the verb *be*.
When the verb is correct, the subject of the sentence and the
verb match.

Rewrite the postcard. Correct the forms of *be*.

Dear Elena,

    Hello from Iceland. You was right! This vacation
were really amazing. The pufflings is the cutest birds.

    We was outside one night. We heard a small cry.
The sound be very sad. It be a little peep-peep-peep.

    Two little pufflings was stranded in the street. We caught
them in a box. The night were very cold, but we didn't care.
We let the birds go at the beach. They was so happy
near the ocean. We was happy too.

      See you soon,

      Marcia

_____

_____

_____

_____

_____

_____

_____

_____

_____

_____

Name _____

Taking Notes

Read this passage to find out more about Iceland.

The Land of the Midnight Sun

Iceland is a country that is also a large island. It is very far north, close to the Arctic Circle, in the North Atlantic Ocean. For two months in the winter, it is dark all the time, except for four to six hours of light a day. But in June, it is daylight all the time. There is no night at all. That is why Iceland is called "The Land of the Midnight Sun."

Even though Iceland is very far north, it is not as cold as you might expect. Most people in Iceland live on the coast. Warm winds from the sea keep the coast from getting very cold. The winters are mild compared to the winters in the northern United States and Canada. The summers in Iceland are cool. The temperature is more like spring than the hot summers most Americans and Canadians are used to.

Take notes on the passage and write them in the outline below.

Iceland

What is it? _____

Where is it? _____

Why is it called "The Land of the Midnight Sun"? _____

_____

_____

What is the weather like? _____

_____

Name _____

Choosing What's Important

Read this passage. Then answer the questions below.

Natural Wonders of Iceland

The inner part of Iceland has few people but many wonders of nature.

Volcanoes A volcano is an opening in the earth over very hot melted rock. It gives off a gas that pushes up through the opening and makes a big explosion. *Iceland has over 200 volcanoes.*

Geysers Geysers are hot springs that throw streams of water into the air. The word *geyser* comes from *Geysir,* the most famous natural fountain in Iceland.

A trip to Iceland would show you many wonders of nature.

1. What do the two subheadings tell about the title?

_____

2. Look at the last sentence under "Volcanoes." Why

do you think it is in slanted letters? _____

_____

3. Which two words appear in slanted type under "Geysers"? Why?

_____

4. What does the picture show? _____

_____

5. What information is repeated in the last paragraph? _____

_____

Name _____

Revising Your Research Report

**Reread your story. What do you need to make it better?
Use this page to help you decide. Put a checkmark in the
box for each sentence that describes your personal narrative.**

Rings the Bell!

☐ I chose an interesting topic to research.

☐ I used different sources to find information on the topic.

☐ My paragraphs have topic sentences and supporting facts.

☐ My ending sums up what I found out.

☐ There are almost no mistakes.

Getting Stronger

☐ I could make the topic more interesting for the reader.

☐ More sources would make sure I have the facts right.

☐ I could add some supporting details to my paragraphs.

☐ I need a better ending.

☐ There are a few mistakes.

Try Harder

☐ My topic isn't very interesting.

☐ I didn't use enough sources to find my facts.

☐ I don't have topic sentences for my paragraphs, and I'm
missing many supporting details.

☐ There are a lot of mistakes.

Name _____

Subject-Verb Agreement

Circle the correct form of each verb.

1. Lizards (is/are) the largest group in the reptile family.

2. The Komodo dragon (is/are) the largest lizard.

3. The Komodo dragon (measure/measures) up to 10 feet in length.

4. Lizards (lives/live) in every kind of habitat except the ocean.

5. All reptiles (are/is) cold-blooded.

6. A cold-blooded animal (do/does) not make its own body heat.

7. To warm its blood, a lizard (bask/basks) in the sun.

8. I (own/owns) a lizard called a swift.

9. The swift (move/moves) slowly when it is cold.

10. Then I (turn/turns) on a heat lamp.

11. Suddenly, the swift (runs/run) very fast.

12. At night, lizards (hide/hides) to stay away from enemies.

Spelling Words

Look for spelling patterns you have learned to help you remember the Spelling Words on this page. Think about the parts that you find hard to spell.

Write the missing letters in the Spelling Words below.

1. c ____ ____ ____ d

2. ____ lot

3. b ____ y

4. ____ ____ r

5. w ____ ____ ____ d

6. n ____ ____

7. ____ ____ o

8. g ____ ____ l

9. w ____ nt

10. in ____ ____

11. w ____ ____

12. th ____ ____

Study List On another sheet of paper, write each Spelling Word. Check the list to be sure you spell each word correctly.

Spelling Words

1. girl
2. they
3. want
4. was
5. into
6. who
7. our
8. new
9. would
10. could
11. a lot
12. buy

Name _____

Spelling Spree

Opposites Switch Write the Spelling Word that means the opposite of each underlined word or words.

1–2. I <u>wouldn't</u> be able to run much faster if I <u>couldn't</u> find a pair of shoes that fit.

3–4. The <u>old</u> parents named their baby <u>boy</u> Sue.

5–6. It takes a <u>little</u> of money to <u>sell</u> a boat that big.

7–8. I <u>wasn't</u> going <u>out</u> of the park when I saw smoke coming from a nearby house.

1–2. _____

3–4. _____

5–6. _____

7–8. _____

Spelling Words

1. girl
2. they
3. want
4. was
5. into
6. who
7. our
8. new
9. would
10. could
11. a lot
12. buy

Letter Math Add and subtract letters from the words below to make Spelling Words. Write the new words.

9. out – t + r = _____

10. then – n + y = _____

11. while – ile + o = _____

12. slant – sl + w = _____

Name _____

Proofreading and Writing

Proofreading Circle the four misspelled Spelling Words in this announcement. Then write each word correctly.

Spelling Words

1. girl
2. they
3. want
4. was
5. into
6. who
7. our
8. new
9. would
10. could
11. a lot
12. buy

The State Zoo is proud to announce a noo approach to exhibiting our animals. Each animal's home is now more like the habitat thay would find in the wild. We think that the change will make alot of difference in the lives of the animals. And after all, we wont the animals to feel that this is their home!

1. _____   3. _____

2. _____   4. _____

Describe a Habitat Draw a picture of an animal in its habitat. Then write a few sentences describing what you drew. The animal can be real or imaginary. Use Spelling Words from the list.

Name _____

Beach Crossword

Complete the crossword puzzle using the words from the box.

Across

2. a dock
3. dived downward
4. rested in warmth
6. a long, rolling wave
7. the line where earth and sky meet

Down

1. struck against powerfully
5. sea animal with fur and flippers
6. waves, or to ride on waves

Vocabulary

basked
buffeted
horizon
quay
surf
swell
seal
swooped

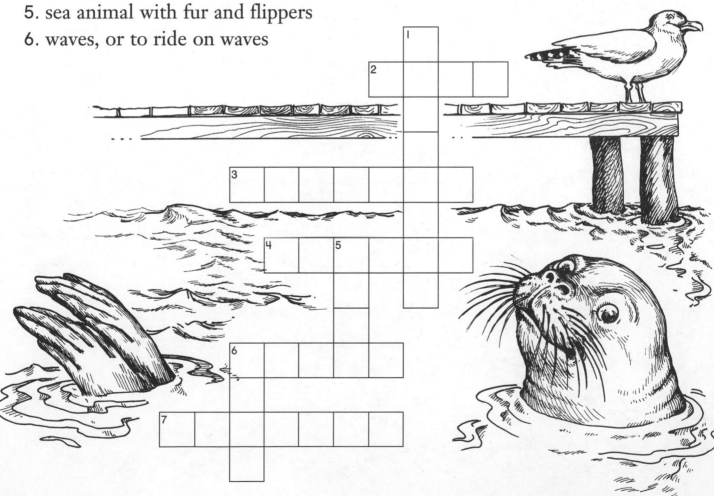

Theme 4: **Animal Habitats**   23

Name _____

Venn Diagram

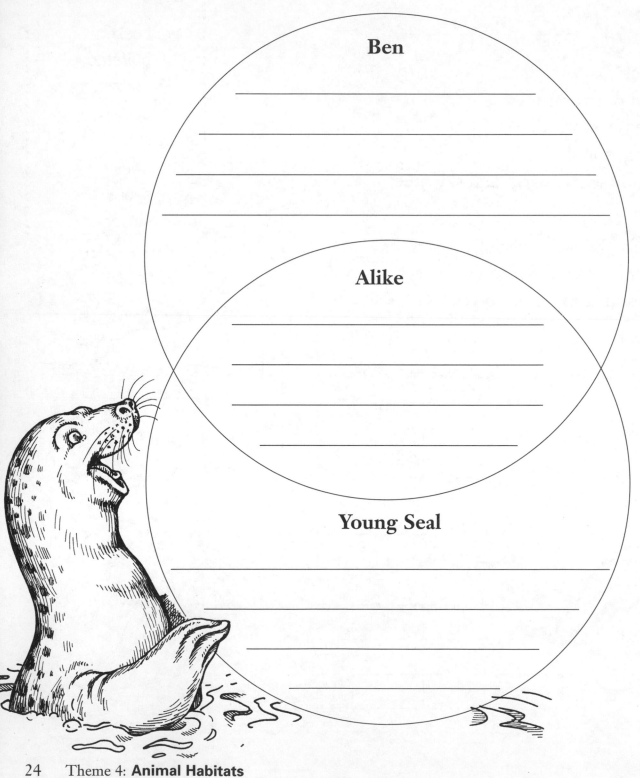

Ben

_____

_____

_____

Alike

_____

_____

_____

_____

Young Seal

_____

_____

_____

Name _____

Ben's Diary

Suppose Ben kept a diary. Help him finish this page by completing the sentences with details from *Seal Surfer*.

One day when Granddad and I were on the beach, we

found _____.

That summer I watched as _____

_____. All winter, my young

seal friend _____.

When spring came, I thought my seal friend _____

_____. Then she returned one summer day

when I was surfing. When I started to drown, she helped me by

_____.

I knew we would be friends forever!

Name _____

Different and Alike

Read the story. Then complete the diagram on the next page.

Which Kind to Choose?

When Linda and Tracy learned they could each get a dog, the two friends found the dog books in the library. Then they started reading. Some time later, Linda said, "I'd like a dog that's friendly, loving, and loyal. Oh, and you know, my great-grandmother lives with us. She can't get out much, so we want a small dog to sit with her in the day. Also, it shouldn't need too much outdoor exercise."

Tracy said, "This book says toy poodles don't need a lot of exercise. They're also loving and like to be cuddled. And they need to be brushed every day."

"A small poodle sounds perfect for my family," Linda said. "What kind of dog is your family looking for?"

"You've seen how big our yard is," Tracy responded. "And my family loves to hike, so we're looking for a big dog that enjoys the outdoors and can keep up with us!"

"How about a Labrador retriever?" asked Linda. "It says that they love the outdoors, long walks, and exercise. They don't need as much grooming as other dogs."

"They're beautiful," Tracy said, looking at the picture. "My family would love one. But I wonder if they're friendly and loyal."

"It says they are," Linda said, looking at the book.

The girls smiled at each other and talked about dogs for hours! Which dog did each one choose? Guess!

Name _____

Different and Alike continued

Complete the diagram with details from the story.

Toy Poodles

_____

_____

_____

Similarities

_____

_____

_____

Labrador Retrievers

_____

_____

_____

Which dog would you choose — a poodle or a Labrador retriever? Why?

_____

_____

Name _____

Happy Endings

**Complete the story by filling in the blanks. Build each word by
adding either _-ed_ or _-ing_ to the word in dark type. Remember,
when a base word ends with a consonant and _y_, change the
_y_ to _i_ before adding _-ed_.**

As Ellie walked beneath the maple tree, she heard a noise from

above. Ellie **(look)** _____ up and spotted a nest

with two baby robins inside. The young birds **(cry)**

_____ out, "Cheep! Cheep!"

"Why are you crying?" Ellie asked the noisy birds. She **(try)**

_____ to figure out the problem. "Are you

hungry?" she wondered.

"Cheep! Cheep!" the birds **(reply)** _____.

Ellie **(start)** _____ **(worry)** _____

that the mother robin would not return. She hoped the mother bird was

(hurry) _____ back with food.

Suddenly, the mother robin appeared. She

(empty) _____ a beak full of worms into the

mouths of her hungry babies. The young birds began **(chirp)**

_____ sweetly. It was very **(satisfy)**

_____ to see the birds so happy.

Name _____

Adding Endings

A **base word** is a word to which an ending may be added. When a base word ends with *e*, drop the *e* before adding *-ed* or *-ing*. When a base word ends with one vowel and one consonant, the consonant is usually doubled before *-ed* or *-ing* is added.

care − e + ed = car**ed**   grin + n + ing = gri**nning**

▶ In the starred word *fixing*, the *x* in *fix* is not doubled before *-ing* is added.

When a base word ends with a consonant and *y*, change the *y* to *i* before adding *-es* or *-ed*.

baby − y + ies = bab**ies**

Write each Spelling Word under the heading that shows what happens to the base word when an ending is added.

Spelling Words

1. cared
2. babies
3. chopped
4. saving
5. carried
6. fixing*
7. hurried
8. joking
9. grinning
10. smiled
11. wrapped
12. parties

Final e Dropped

_____

_____

_____

_____

y Changed to i

_____

_____

_____

_____

Final Consonant Doubled

_____

_____

_____

No Spelling Change

_____

_____

_____

- Theme 4: **Animal Habitats**   29

Name _____

Spelling Spree

Words in Words Write the Spelling Words that contain each of the smaller words below.

Example: top _____*stopped*_____

1. king _____
2. rap _____
3. are _____
4. grin _____
5. hop _____
6. mile _____

Spelling Words
1. cared
2. babies
3. chopped
4. saving
5. carried
6. fixing*
7. hurried
8. joking
9. grinning
10. smiled
11. wrapped
12. parties

Classifying Write the Spelling Word that belongs in each group.

Example: forming, creating, _____*making*_____

7. moved, transported, _____
8. infants, toddlers, _____
9. repairing, mending, _____
10. raced, rushed, _____
11. celebrations, get-togethers, _____
12. keeping, storing, _____

7. _____   10. _____
8. _____   11. _____
9. _____   12. _____

Name _____

Proofreading and Writing

Proofreading Circle the five misspelled Spelling Words in the following journal entry. Then write each word correctly.

October 10—I fished all morning. Then I hurryed back to the harbor to meet Ben. We saw a female seal swimming in the harbor water. She looked like she was grining at us. I choped up some fish and tossed it to her. The seal ate the fish right away. Ben smiled and said, "I guess she's not interested in saveing the fish for later." The seal swam away. We wraped up the rest of our fish and brought it home. I wonder if we'll see that seal again.

Spelling Words

1. cared
2. babies
3. chopped
4. saving
5. carried
6. fixing*
7. hurried
8. joking
9. grinning
10. smiled
11. wrapped
12. parties

1. _____   4. _____

2. _____   5. _____

3. _____

Write About an Animal Do you have a favorite animal story? Maybe you know a funny story about a pet. Perhaps you have seen a rare or unusual animal in a zoo or aquarium. Maybe you have read a book or seen a TV program about an animal that did something remarkable.

On a separate sheet of paper, write a paragraph about an interesting animal. Use Spelling Words from the list.

Name _____

Find the Right Word, the Right Meaning

Read each sentence. Then choose the correct meaning of the underlined word from the dictionary definitions below. Write the number of the correct entry and the correct meaning next to the sentence.

bit [1] *noun* **1.** A tiny piece: *I ate the last bit of fish.* **2.** A small amount of time: *The train will come in a bit.* **3.** A small role, as in a play.
bit [1] (bĭt) ◇ *noun, plural* **bits**
bit [2] *noun* **1.** A drilling tool. **2.** The metal mouthpiece of a bridle, used to control a horse.
bit [2] (bĭt) ◇ *noun, plural* **bits**
bit [3] *verb* Past tense and a past participle of **bite.**
bit [3] (bĭt) ◇ *verb*

1. The rider put the <u>bit</u> and the saddle on the horse.

   _____

2. I'll go to the movies with you in a <u>bit</u>.

   _____

3. The wood was so hard that it snapped the carpenter's <u>bit</u>.

   _____

4. We <u>bit</u> into the sweet apples.

   _____

5. There was just a <u>bit</u> of salad left after dinner.

   _____

Name _____

Finding Helping Verbs

Circle the helping verb in each sentence. Underline the verb that it is helping.

1. Ben has watched the seals.

2. We have listened to the waves.

3. The waves have buffeted the seals.

4. The seals have arrived safely.

5. Grandfather has talked with Ben.

6. He has explained many mysteries of the sea.

7. The waves have crashed into the shore.

8. One seal has rescued Ben.

9. She has helped him.

10. You have learned about seals.

Name _____

Completing with Helping Verbs

Write *have* or *has* to complete each sentence.

1. We _____ learned about seals.

2. Seals _____ basked in the sun.

3. It _____ warmed the seals.

4. Grandfather _____ played Beethoven for seals.

5. They _____ listened to the music.

6. Ben _____ surfed with seals.

7. He _____ watched one of the seals grow up.

8. She _____ returned every year.

9. I _____ enjoyed learning about seals.

10. You _____ discovered many new facts.

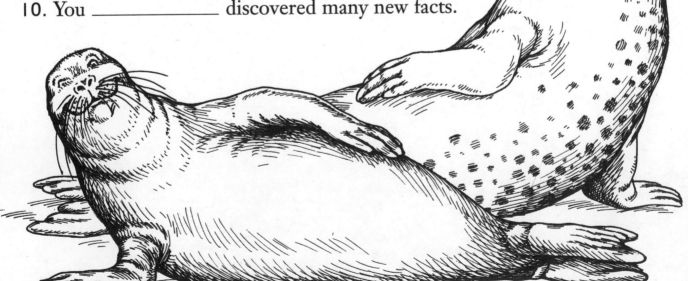

Sentence Combining with Helping Verbs

Use helping verbs to combine each pair of sentences.

1. We have studied seals. We have discovered how they live.

   _____

2. A storm has started. A storm has threatened some seals.

   _____

3. The seals have dived deep. The seals have escaped.

   _____

4. Ben's seal has returned. Ben's seal has recognized him right away.

   _____

5. The waves have pushed Ben off his board. The waves have
   pulled him under.

   _____

6. A seal has pushed Ben up. A seal has saved him.

   _____

7. I have finished the story. I have cried at the ending.

   _____

8. Grandfather and Ben have watched the seals. Grandfather
   and Ben have admired the seals.

   _____

Name _____

Planning a Poem

Use this graphic organizer to plan a poem of your own.
Then write a poem about an experience you have had with
an animal, or a place that you like very much.

Sense Words
I Might Use

_____

_____

_____

Unusual Comparisons
I Might Use

_____

_____

_____

What Is the Big Picture I Want to Create?

_____

_____

_____

Rhythm Patterns
I Might Use

_____

_____

_____

How I Might
Organize the Poem

_____

_____

_____

Name _____

Using Exact Verbs

Good writers try not to use a gencral verb when they can choose
an exact verb to describe an action. Read these examples:

Wildflowers appeared on the rugged cliffs.
Wildflowers **bloomed** on the rugged cliffs.

The rough waves threw the seals against the rocks.
The rough waves **dashed** the seals against the rocks.

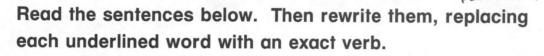

**Read the sentences below. Then rewrite them, replacing
each underlined word with an exact verb.**

1. The face of the seal suddenly <u>showed</u> through the water.

   _____

   _____

2. The seal's shiny body <u>swam</u> in the water.

   _____

   _____

3. The boy's body <u>dropped</u> into the darkness of the sea.

   _____

   _____

4. The boy <u>moved head over heels</u> through the surf.

   _____

5. The seal <u>put</u> the boy onto his surfboard.

   _____

Name _____

Oh, Deer!

You are a scientist observing a small group of deer.
The deer are eating grass in a field near a forest of
trees. Deer have never been seen in this field before.
Use the Vocabulary Words to write sentences about
the deer. If you need help, use your glossary.

Vocabulary

grazing
population
starve
surrounding
territory
wander

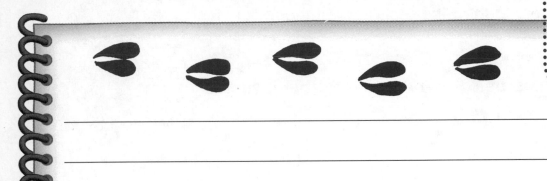

Name _____

Decision Chart

Problem: _____

_____

_____

Do you agree with how the characters solve the problem?	
Yes, when...	*No*, when...
_____	_____
_____	_____
_____	_____
_____	_____
_____	_____
_____	_____
_____	_____
_____	_____
_____	_____
_____	_____
_____	_____
_____	_____

Name _____

Oh, Deer Me!

Write the following story events on the lines below in the order they occurred.

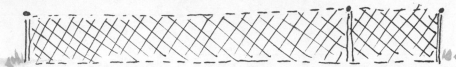

The neighbors begin a peaceful protest.

Sonia sleeps outside with the deer.

Papa calls the animal control officer.

The wildlife rescuer takes the deer away.

Deer appear in the garden.

The Pigeon Lady teaches Sonia and Peach about deer.

The neighbors order pizza.

Mr. Benny calls the wildlife rescue organization.

1. _____

2. _____

3. _____

4. _____

5. _____

6. _____

7. _____

8. _____

What's Best for the Neighbors?

All the neighbors must decide what to plant in the neighborhood garden. Read the dialogue. Then answer the questions on the next page.

Mrs. Rhonda: Let's grow tomatoes again. They can be canned, and we can freeze tomato sauce.

Luis: Sure, and everyone likes pizza sauce. I vote for potatoes as well. If we store them in a cool place, we can use them all winter.

Blossom: But potatoes are so cheap to buy at the store! They take too much room. I'd rather have more space for lettuce and spinach.

Mr. Yost: But I don't like spinach.

Blossom: We can plant beans and peas around the fence. That's easy enough. Then the center can be used for lettuce, spinach, and tomatoes.

Mrs. Rhonda: Shall we plant squash this year?

Luis: Squash always takes over the garden. If we plant three zucchini plants, we'll have thousands of zucchini, and we'll never use it all. It's a waste.

Mr. Yost: But zucchini bread tastes good.

Mrs. Rhonda: Here's an idea. We'll plant just one zucchini plant over here, and we can set potatoes all around it. That way, all the vines will be in the same area. Then we can plant the salad greens together and the peas and beans together too.

Name _____

What's Best for the Neighbors? continued

Answer each question about the neighborhood meeting.

1. What good points does Mrs. Rhonda make in favor of planting tomatoes?

   _____

2. What good point does Luis make in favor of planting potatoes?

   _____

3. What two good points does Blossom make against growing potatoes?

   _____

4. Whose points are not well backed by facts?

   _____

5. Do you agree with Mrs. Rhonda's ideas for the garden? Why or why not?

   _____

   _____

Name _____

What's the Word?

Prefix	Meaning	Example
un-	"not" or "the opposite of"	unable
re-	"again" or "back to"	rebuild

Suffix	Meaning	Example
-ful	"full of" or "having the qualities of"	cheerful
-er	"one who"	teacher
-ly	"in this way"	gently

Read each clue and unscramble the answer.

1. fill again: **LELRIF** _____

2. in a kind way: **DLNKYI** _____

3. someone who announces: **NEURNACON** _____

4. not clear: **ACNRLEU** _____

5. full of beauty: **LABUTUFIE** _____

6. appear again: **PERAEPRA** _____

7. full of help: **HPLELUF** _____

8. someone who sings: **NIRSEG** _____

9. the opposite of sure: **URESUN** _____

10. in a soft way: **LYFTOS** _____

Name _____

Prefixes and Suffixes (*re-, un-; -ful, -ly, -er*)

A **prefix** is a word part added to the beginning of a base word. It adds meaning to the base word.

Prefix		Base Word		New Word	Meaning
re-	+	make	=	**re**make	to make again
un-	+	happy	=	**un**happy	not happy

A **suffix** is a word part added to the end of a base word. It also adds meaning to the base word.

Base Word		Suffix		New Word	Meaning
care	+	-ful	=	care**ful**	full of care
friend	+	-ly	=	friend**ly**	in a friendly way
help	+	-er	=	help**er**	one who helps

Write each Spelling Word under its prefix or suffix.

Spelling Words

1. helper
2. unfair
3. friendly
4. unhappy
5. remake
6. careful
7. hopeful
8. unlike
9. retell
10. sadly
11. farmer
12. unhurt

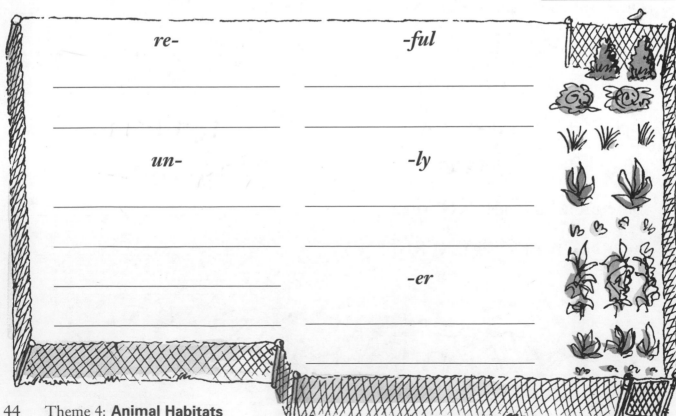

re-

_____

_____

un-

_____

_____

-ful

_____

-ly

_____

-er

_____

Spelling Spree

Base Word Hunt Write a Spelling Word that has the
same base word as each word below.

1. friendship _____

2. sadness _____

3. helpful _____

4. likely _____

5. fairness _____

Prefix and Suffix Addition Write Spelling Words by
adding *re-, un-, -ful,* or *-er* to the words below.

6. tell _____

7. care _____

8. happy _____

9. hope _____

10. makc _____

11. hurt _____

12. farm _____

Theme 4: **Animal Habitats**   45

Name _____

Proofreading and Writing

Proofreading Circle the five misspelled Spelling Words in the report. Then write each word correctly.

Wildlife Rescue Report

Today I answered a call from a group of friendly neighbors in the city. Several deer had wandered into a backyard. The animal control officer arrived, but the people were (onhappy) about what he proposed to do. I came with no (helpper), but I managed to get the deer onto my truck. The animals were all (unhurte). A (farrmer) helped me herd the deer into the woods. I am (hopful) that they will not wander back to the city again.

1. _farmer_ 4. _hopeful_

2. _unhappy_ 5. _unhurt_

3. _helper_

✏️ **Write a Letter** How would you thank Carl Jackson if you were Sonia?

On a separate sheet of paper, write a letter thanking Mr. Jackson for rescuing the deer. Tell him what you hope happens to the deer. Use Spelling Words from the list.

Name _____

Which Form Is It?

**Read each sentence. Decide which inflected form of the
base word shown in parentheses belongs in the sentence.
Then write the word in the blank.**

easy *adjective* Needing very little effort; not hard.
    adjective **easier, easiest**

nod *verb* To move the head down and then up in a quick motion.
    noun A nodding motion.
    verb **nodded, nodding**   *noun, plural* **nods**

rumble *verb* To make or move with a deep, long rolling sound.
    noun A deep, long rolling sound.
    verb **rumbled, rumbling**   *noun, plural* **rumbles**

study *noun* The act or process of learning. **2.** A branch of knowledge.
    verb **1.** To try to learn. **2.** To examine closely and carefully.
    noun, plural **studies**   *verb* **studied, studying**

1. The deer were **(nod)** _____
   their heads sleepily.

2. The first truck that **(rumble)** _____
   down the street was a delivery van.

3. Saving deer is not the **(easy)** _____
   task, but it's worth the effort.

4. Clarence said, "We **(study)** _____
   deer in science last year."

5. The wildlife rescuer **(nod)** _____
   in greeting.

6. Sonia felt sad as the truck was **(rumble)** _____
   away with the deer.

Name _____

Using Irregular Verbs

Complete each sentence with the correct form of the verb in parentheses.

1. One morning, Sonia _____ an amazing sight.
   (see, past)

2. Five deer had _____ into her yard.
   (come, with *had*)

3. The deer _____ the carrot. (eat, past)

4. The neighbors _____ to see the animals.
   (come, past)

5. Mr. Benny has _____ deer in the wild.
   (see, with *has*)

6. By morning, the deer had _____ a lot of flowers.
   (eat, with *had*)

7. We have _____ everything we can.
   (did, with *have*)

8. The wildlife rescuer _____ to catch the deer.
   (go, past)

9. He _____ his job very well. (do, past)

10. The van with the deer has _____ to the country.

    (go, with *has*)

Name _____

Completing Sentences with Irregular Verbs

Complete each sentence with the correct form of the verb in parentheses.

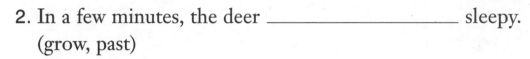

1. The wildlife rescuer _____ the deer medicine to make it tired. (give, past)

2. In a few minutes, the deer _____ sleepy. (grow, past)

3. The man _____ the deer away from the city. (take, past)

4. The neighbors had _____ many photographs of the deer. (took, with *had*).

5. The deer have _____ happily in their new home. (run, with *have*)

6. The young deer have _____ a lot since they were born. (grow, with *have*)

7. A reporter _____ about the deer in Sonia's yard. (write, past)

8. He has _____ the story to his editor. (give, with *has*)

9. Sonia _____ to show the article to her friends. (run, past)

10. She has _____ a poem about the deer. (write, with *has*)

Name _____

Using the Correct Verb Form

**Read each sentence. If the verb is correct,
write C after the sentence. If the verb is incorrect,
rewrite the sentence with the correct form.**

1. A squirrel comed into Sonia's house.

   _____

2. It has eated a box of crackers.

   _____

3. Sonia runned to tell her parents about the squirrel.

   _____

4. They saw the cracker crumbs in the kitchen.

   _____

5. The squirrel had ran out the window.

   _____

6. They wented to the yard.

   _____

7. The squirrel went up a tree.

   _____

8. Sonia has seed the squirrel again.

   _____

Name _____

Problem-Solution Planner

Use this page to help you plan a problem-solution essay. Work with a partner. Think of a problem and two ideas to solve it. Tell what happened with each idea. End with a sentence or two that tells how the problem was solved.

Problem:

_____

Solution Idea #1:

_____

_____

Solution Idea #2:

_____

_____

What happened:

_____

_____

_____

What happened:

_____

_____

_____

Problem Solved!

_____

_____

Theme 4: **Animal Habitats**   51

Name _____

Varying Sentence Types

Writers use the four kinds of sentences to make
their writing more interesting.

▶ A **statement** tells something and ends with a period:
   Deer live in the woods.

▶ A **question** asks something and ends with a
   question mark: Do deer live in the woods?

▶ An **exclamation** shows surprise or another
   strong feeling and ends with an exclamation point:

   Deer visited the city!

▶ A **command** tells someone to do something and ends
   with a period: Take the deer back to the woods.

**Rewrite each sentence as directed. You may need to
add, remove, or reorder words to change sentence types.**

1. They will think of a way to help the deer.

   Command: _____

2. Are wild animals safe in the city?

   Exclamation: _____

3. Call the animal control officers.

   Statement: _____

4. What do you see out the window?

   Command: _____

5. There are four deer in the garden.

   Question: _____

Name _____

Vocabulary Items

Use the test-taking strategies and tips you have learned to help you answer these vocabulary items. This practice will help you when you take this kind of test.

Read each sentence. Choose the word that means about the same as the underlined word. Fill in the circle for the correct answer at the bottom of the page.

1 The sky was <u>speckled</u> with millions of puffins returning to the island.

(A) spotted

(B) noisy

(C) striped

(D) quiet

2 The birds came to the <u>uninhabited</u> islands to lay their eggs and raise their chicks.

(F) crowded

(G) treeless

(H) dangerous

(J) deserted

3 The puffins make <u>burrows</u> underground for their nests.

(A) caves

(B) tunnels

(C) hills

(D) waterways

ANSWER ROWS   1 (A) (B) (C) (D)   3 (A) (B) (C) (D)
              2 (F) (G) (H) (J)

Name _____

Vocabulary Items continued

4 The puffins were <u>bobbing</u> up and down on the waves of the sea.

(F) walking

(G) bouncing

(H) sinking

(J) jumping

5 Arnar <u>spies</u> a puffin flying overhead and tells Halla to look.

(A) sees

(B) hides

(C) catches

(D) touches

6 Halla and her friends help pufflings that are <u>stranded</u> on land.

(F) lost

(G) living

(H) stuck

(J) sleeping

ANSWER ROWS	4 (F) (G) (H) (J)	6 (F) (G) (H) (J)
	5 (A) (B) (C) (D)	

Name _____

Spelling Review

Write Spelling Words from the list on this page to answer the questions.

1–8. Which eight words have the vowel + *r* sound in *hair*?

1. _____   5. _____

2. _____   6. _____

3. _____   7. _____

4. _____   8. _____

9–16. Which eight words have endings that have changed the spelling of the base word?

9. _____   13. _____

10. _____   14. _____

11. _____   15. _____

12. _____   16. _____

17–21. Which five words have the prefix *re-* or *un-*?

17. _____   20. _____

18. _____   21. _____

19. _____

22–25. Which four words have the suffix *-ful*, *-ly*, or *-er*?

22. _____   24. _____

23. _____   25. _____

Name _____

Spelling Spree

Wacky Rhymes Write a Spelling Word in each sentence that rhymes with the underlined word.

1. I will wear a _____ of new socks to the <u>fair</u>.

2. Who got <u>hair</u> on my good _____?

3. She's _____ because our team is <u>winning</u>.

4. They are _____ and <u>poking</u> at piñatas.

5. When my parents got <u>married</u>, my mother _____ roses.

Riddle Time Write a Spelling Word to answer each question.

6. What do you blow into a balloon? _____

7. What is a yellow or green fruit that grows on trees? _____

8. What do you do if you recite a story again? _____

9. How does somebody wearing a frown feel? _____

10. What has been done to a cut-up apple? _____

11. Who are the youngest people? _____

12. What events can you go to on birthdays? _____

Name _____

Proofreading and Writing

Proofreading Circle the six misspelled Spelling
Words in this story. Then write each word correctly.

Marv, the farm helpir, worked hard and caired for

some baby rabbits that were unliek others because they

were very small. He would reemake their beds in his

freindly way. Marv was hopefull they would grow

stronger soon.

1. _____   4. _____

2. _____   5. _____

3. _____   6. _____

Spelling Words

1. care
2. friendly
3. smiled
4. unlike
5. sadly
6. scare
7. bare
8. grinning
9. helper
10. cared
11. remake
12. bear
13. hopeful
14. unhurt

Tale of a Bear Use Spelling Words to complete
this story beginning.

Mimi watched the polar 7. _____ cub. His

8. _____ head made her shiver. Mimi looked at the cub

9. _____. Mimi's dad knew that she wanted to take

10. _____ of the cub. He told her it was 11. _____

by the cold, and icebergs didn't 12. _____ it. Then Mimi

13. _____ happily. She even started 14. _____.

✏️ **Write a Description** On a separate sheet of paper, write about your
favorite animal and where it lives. Use the Spelling Review Words.

Name _____

Voyagers

If you were to take a voyage, where would you go? Describe the place and tell why you would go there.

_____

_____

_____

_____

_____

_____

_____

_____

Would you go alone or with other people? What things would you bring with you?

_____

_____

_____

_____

Name _____

Voyagers

Fill in the chart as you read the stories.

	Across the Wide Dark Sea	Yunmi and Halmoni's Trip	Trapped by the Ice!
Who takes the voyage? **Where does the voyage begin and end?**			
What qualities help the voyagers succeed?			

Tale of a Sea Voyage

**On the line after each sentence, write
the correct definition of the underlined word.**

Definitions You Will Need:

► heavy metal object that keeps a ship in place
► crowded
► trip from one place to another
► passing slowly through small openings
► small community in a new place
► stay alive
► tired

1. In 1620, the Pilgrims made a long <u>journey</u> from England to

   America. _____

2. With so many people, the ship was <u>cramped</u>. _____

3. Water kept <u>seeping</u> through the wooden walls of the ship.

   _____

4. When the ship neared land, the crew dropped the <u>anchor</u>.

   _____

5. The many hardships made the Pilgrims <u>weary</u>. _____

6. Even though the voyage was very difficult, all but one of the passengers

   managed to <u>survive</u>. _____

7. After the Pilgrims landed, they chose a spot and built a <u>settlement</u>.

   _____

Inference Chart

1. How does the boy feel when the journey begins?

Story Clues (pages 113–115)	**What I Know**
He looks ahead at the wide dark sea. _____ _____	_____ _____ _____

My Inference _____

2. How does the boy feel after six weeks at sea?

Story Clues (pages 116–119)	**What I Know**
_____ _____	_____ _____

My Inference _____

3. How do the people react to the report of the new land?

Story Clues (pages 122-124)	**What I Know**
_____ _____	_____ _____

My Inference _____

Name _____

Report on the Journey

**Use a complete sentence to answer each
question about *Across the Wide Dark Sea*.**

1. What are some things the Pilgrims bring with them on the

   Mayflower? _____

   _____

2. Why does the boy tire of being on the ship week after week? _____

   _____

3. What serious damage does one storm do to the *Mayflower*? _____

   _____

4. Why do the people on the *Mayflower* make the dangerous journey?

   _____

5. What do the people fear when they want to go ashore? _____

   _____

6. Where do the Pilgrims decide to start their new settlement?

   _____

7. What are some of the things the Indians teach the Pilgrims? _____

   _____

8. How do the boy and his father feel about the new settlement in the

   spring? _____

Name _____

Making Good Guesses

**Read the story. Then answer the questions on
the next page.**

A Trip Back in Time!

When Dad said we were going to Plymouth to see where
the Pilgrims lived, Mom looked at us sharply. She said, "I want
you two to behave and learn something today." My sister
Margie smiled and winked at me when Mom looked away.

The place was not at all what we expected. Instead of a
museum display, we found ourselves walking past full-sized
homes with fences and gardens. It looked like New Plymouth
might have looked in 1627. People who dressed and talked like
Pilgrims answered our questions as they went about their tasks
for the day. It seemed as if we had been carried back in time.

The best part of our visit happened by chance. We were
looking at the goats when a young Pilgrim girl came by
with a bucket of water. She told us how the brown goat
had kicked her last week. Then she invited us into her
home, which turned out to be a small, cramped, hot,
smoky cottage with a cooking fire right on the dirt floor.
It was as if we'd made a new friend. We learned all about
Mary, how she did chores most of the day, how she
hated to milk goats, how she loved to
shine the kettle with salt and vinegar.
And she was so polite to all the
adults! Why, she even curtsied to
my parents. Needless to say, we
were too busy talking to get into
trouble — well, on that day anyway!

Making Good Guesses continued

**Use clues from the story and what you know
to answer each question.**

1. What was Margie planning to do?

   _____

Story Clues	**What I Know**
_____	_____
_____	_____

2. How does the storyteller feel about the Pilgrim girl's home?

   _____

Story Clues	**What I Know**
_____	_____
_____	_____

3. What does the storyteller realize about the life of a Pilgrim girl?

   _____

Story Clues	**What I Know**
_____	_____
_____	_____

Name _____

Riddled with Suffixes

**Each word below contains a base word and a suffix.
Write each base word. Put only one letter on each
line. To solve the riddle, write each numbered letter
on the line with the matching number below.**

1. darkness — — — —
                4

2. kindness — — — —
                9

3. sunless   — — — —
                  7

4. careless — — — — — —
                5

5. hopeless — — — — — —
               6   3

6. worthless — — — — —
               1

7. goodness — — — —
                 2

8. emptiness — — — — —

9. priceless — — — — — — —
                         8

10. fearless — — — — —

Native Americans shared more than their food with the
settlers. They also shared their language. Solve the puzzle
to learn one Native American word we use in English.

— — — — — — — — —
1 2 3 4 5 6 7 8 9

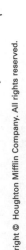

Name _____

The Vowel Sounds in
tooth and *cook*

When you hear the /o͞o/ sound, as in *tooth* or *chew*, remember that it may be spelled with the pattern *oo* or *ew*. The /o͝o/ sound, as in *cook*, may be spelled with the pattern *oo*.

/o͞o/ tooth, chew

/o͝o/ cook

▶ In the starred words *shoe* and *blue*, the /o͞o/ sound is spelled *oe* or *ue*.

Write each Spelling Word under its vowel sound.

Spelling Words

1. tooth
2. chew
3. grew
4. cook
5. shoe*
6. blue*
7. boot
8. flew
9. shook
10. balloon
11. drew
12. spoon

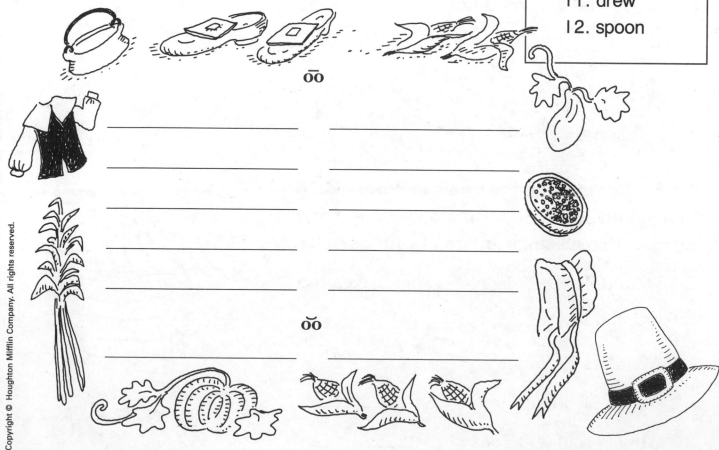

o͞o

_____   _____

_____   _____

_____   _____

_____   _____

o͝o

_____   _____

Theme 5: **Voyagers**   67

Name _____

Spelling Spree

Puzzle Play Write a Spelling Word to fit each clue.

Spelling Words

1. tooth
2. chew
3. grew
4. cook
5. shoe*
6. blue*
7. boot
8. flew
9. shook
10. balloon
11. drew
12. spoon

1. a color __ ☐ __ __

2. a toy you blow up __ ☐ __ __ __ __

3. not a fork or a knife __ __ __ __ ☐

4. past tense of *draw* ☐ __ __ __

5. a dentist works on it __ __ __ __ ☐

6. to prepare food by heating __ ☐ ☐ __ __

What two words might someone on a ship be glad to hear? To find out, write the boxed letters in order.

__ __ __ __ __ __!

Name Game Write the Spelling Word hidden in each name. Look for *o*'s and *w*'s to find the words. Use all small letters in your answers.

Example: Dr. Diego O. Delgado **good**

7. Mr. Jeb O. Otis _____

8. Miss Peg R. Ewing _____

9. Mrs. Peach E. Wild _____

10. Mr. Cash O. O'Krook _____

Name _____

Proofreading and Writing

Proofreading Circle the four misspelled Spelling Words in this diary entry. Then write each word correctly.

This morning, we had fine sailing weather. Never have I seen a sky so clear and blew. Sister and I sat on the deck. We drew pictures of the ship and the sea. Time just floo by! Later, the sails shuk with a sudden wind, and we were sent below. I lost a shue on the stairs as I ran. I will look for it when the storm has passed.

Spelling Words

1. tooth
2. chew
3. grew
4. cook
5. shoe*
6. blue*
7. boot
8. flew
9. shook
10. balloon
11. drew
12. spoon

1. _____

2. _____

3. _____

4. _____

➤ **Write a Travel Poster** The Pilgrims traveled from England to America. Have you taken an interesting trip? Did you travel by ship, car, bus, or plane? What did you see and do?

On a separate sheet of paper, write a travel poster. Make readers want to visit the place you are telling about. Use Spelling Words from the list.

Theme 5: **Voyagers**   69

Name _____

Match Words and Syllables

Use the dictionary entries to answer each question below.

desperate *adjective* **1.** Without or nearly without hope.
2. Ready to run any risk because of feeling hopeless.
des•per•ate (dĕs' pər ĭt) ◊ *adjective*

friend *noun* **1.** A person one knows, likes, and enjoys
being with. **2.** Someone who supports a group, cause, or
movement.
friend (frĕnd) ◊ *noun, plural* **friends**

1. Which word contains one syllable? _____

2. Which word contains three syllables? _____

3. Which word contains one syllable with two vowels? _____

4. What is the first syllable of the word *desperate*? _____

5. Show where the word *desperate* can be hyphenated for word breaks.

_____

Name _____

Using Pronouns for Nouns

**Circle each subject pronoun in the following paragraph.
Then write each pronoun and the verb it matches on the
lines below the paragraph.**

The anchor rises from the sea. It drips water.
Father looks at the ocean. He hopes the journey
will be safe. The sailors cheer. They want the
journey to begin. I hold my mother's hand. We
feel nervous and excited.

1. _____   4. _____

2. _____   5. _____

3. _____

Choose the correct verb to complete each sentence.

6. I _____ the wind in our sail. (watch, watches)

7. It _____ my hair. (blow, blows)

8. We _____ to the sailors. (shout, shouts)

9. They _____ our call. (answer, answers)

10. You _____ the sound of waves. (hear, hears)

Name _____

Replacing Nouns with Pronouns

**Rewrite each sentence. Replace each
underlined subject with a subject pronoun.**

1. The ship drops anchor.

   _____

2. Father points to our new home.

   _____

3. The workers build rough houses.

   _____

4. Mother nurses the sick.

   _____

5. The weather is harsh and dangerous.

   _____

6. My brother and I take care of the young children.

   _____

7. Mother and Father protect our home.

   _____

8. The fields turn green in May.

   _____

9. The sun shines across the land.

   _____

10. Mother, Father, my brother, and I watch the sunrise.

   _____

Name _____

Combining Sentences
with Pronouns

Sentence Combining with Subject Pronouns **Combine
each pair of sentences. Use the word in parentheses.**

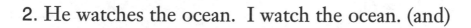

1. You talk to the captain. I talk to the captain. (and)

   _____

2. He watches the ocean. I watch the ocean. (and)

   _____

3. She helps the sailors. I help the sailors. (and)

   _____

4. They sleep on deck. I sleep on deck. (and)

   _____

5. You feel the cold wind. They feel the cold wind. (and)

   _____

6. He raises the sail. I raise the sail. (and)

   _____

7. He steers the boat. She steers the boat. (or)

   _____

8. You will wake up first. She will wake up first. (or)

   _____

9. He builds the house. She builds the house. (and)

   _____

10. You plant the corn. I plant the corn. (or)

    _____

Name _____

Writing a Scene from a Play

Title: The Wide Dark Sea

Scene 1: Time — November 1620
                Place — a beach in the new land

Characters
Thomas — a boy about 8 years old
William — his brother, a boy about 6 years old

What Happens in This Scene

The two boys race up and down the beach. They find clams and mussels and eat them raw. They eat too many and then feel sick.

How the Boys Feel

They are happy to be off the ship. They are excited about the beach. They also are glad to eat fresh food like the clams and mussels. When they feel sick, they are sorry they ate too much.

Play-act with a partner and pretend to be one of the two boys. Act out the events under **What Happens in This Scene**. Remember to show how the boys feel about each event.

**Make notes on this page for dialogue and action ideas. Then
write your scene on another sheet of paper.**

_____

_____

_____

_____

Name _____

Exclamation Points

**Read the play scene. Add exclamation points where
they belong.**

Scene: Place: The Pilgrim settlement on Cape Cod
        Time: A spring day in 1621

Mother: It has been a long, terrible winter. But now it is

    spring. Our family has survived. I am so happy.

Father: Now the children can go outside and play.

    (*The two children run for the door.*) Watch out, Nathan and

    Sarah. You almost knocked over that table.

Nathan: (*excitedly*) The sun is shining. I'll bet it's warm out.

Sarah: (*shouting*) Look, Nathan. There are birds in that tree,

    and they're making a nest.

Mother: Please calm down, children. Eat your breakfast.

    Then you can go out to play.

Father: I am so thankful that we have made it to this new land.

Now write a sentence of your own using an exclamation point.

_____

_____

_____

_____

Name _____

Revising Your Description

Reread your description. What do you need to make it better? Use this page to help you decide. Put a checkmark in the box for each sentence that describes what you have written.

Rings the Bell!

☐ The beginning clearly tells what the description is about.

☐ I describe things in an order that makes sense.

☐ I use sensory words to bring the description to life.

☐ All my sentences are complete.

☐ There are almost no mistakes.

Getting Stronger

☐ I could make clearer what I am describing.

☐ I could order the details in a better way.

☐ I could add more sensory words to bring the description to life.

☐ I need to fix some sentences that aren't complete.

☐ There are a few mistakes.

Try Harder

☐ I forgot to tell what I am describing.

☐ The details are in an order that doesn't make sense.

☐ I haven't used words that help the reader picture what I'm describing.

☐ There are a lot of mistakes.

Name _____

Complete Sentences

Write the words *Complete Sentence* after each complete sentence. Make each incomplete sentence complete by adding words.

1. San Francisco is America's most hilly town.

_____

2. Is located right next to the Golden Gate Bridge.

_____

3. Some of the hills.

_____

4. Going down the hills in a car or cable car can seem scary.

_____

5. Lombard Street goes back and forth and back and forth.

_____

6. Is the crookedest street in the city.

_____

Name _____

Spelling Words

Look for spelling patterns you have learned to help you remember the Spelling Words on this page. Think about the parts that you find hard to spell.

Write the missing letters in the Spelling Words below.

1. d ____ ____ n

2. h ____ ____

3. i ____ ____

4. com ____ ____ ____

5. sto ____ ____ ed

6. st ____ ____ ____ ____ ____

7. ____ ____ ote

8. swi ____ ____ ing

9. fr ____ m

10. ____ ____ ite

11. wri ____ ____ ng

12. br ____ ____ ____ ____ t

──── **Study List** On another sheet of paper, write each Spelling Word. Check the list to be sure you spell each word correctly.

Name _____

Spelling Spree

Find a Rhyme Write a Spelling Word that rhymes with the underlined word.

1. Last <u>night</u> I had to _____ a report on Mars.

2. Jamie _____ home the fish he <u>caught</u>.

3. The statue <u>sits</u> in _____ own room in the museum.

4. Do you know _____ to milk a <u>cow</u>?

5. The teacher _____ me a <u>note</u> to give to my parents.

6. These apples <u>come</u> _____ Washington.

7. I sat _____ in my seat just as a <u>clown</u> came on stage.

Meaning Match Each exercise gives a clue for a word along with an ending. Add the base to the ending to write a Spelling Word. Remember that the spelling of the first word may change.

8. to put words on paper + *ing*

9. to begin + *ed*

10. to move toward the person speaking + *ing*

11. to end + *ed*

12. what you do in a pool + *ing*

Spelling Words

1. down
2. how
3. its
4. coming
5. stopped
6. started
7. wrote
8. swimming
9. from
10. write
11. writing
12. brought

8. _____

9. _____

10. _____

11. _____

12. _____

Theme 5: **Voyagers**   79

Name _____

Proofreading and Writing

Proofreading Circle the four misspelled Spelling Words in this diary entry. Then write each word correctly.

1. down
2. how
3. its
4. coming
5. stopped
6. started
7. wrote
8. swimming
9. from
10. write
11. writing
12. brought

May 3rd

     Things are going pretty well, except that I'm busy with homework. We have to rite a report on an explorer for school. I startted writing mine last week. I was going to finish it on Monday, but we went swiming instead. Now it's due in two days, and I have to figure out howe to finish it on time. I'll be glad when I'm done.

1. _____

2. _____

3. _____

4. _____

✏️ **Write a Round-Robin Story** Get together in a small group with other students. Then write a story about a voyage, with each of you writing one sentence at a time. Use a Spelling Word from the list in each sentence.

Name _____

Travel Words

Match each word with its definition by writing the letter of the definition on the line beside the word. Then choose a vocabulary word from the list to finish each sentence.

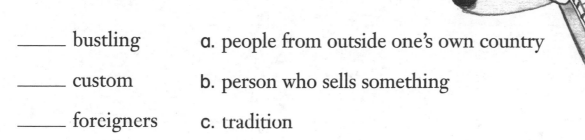

_____ bustling   **a.** people from outside one's own country

_____ custom   **b.** person who sells something

_____ foreigners   **c.** tradition

_____ passport   **d.** paper allowing someone to visit other countries

_____ sightseeing   **e.** busy

_____ vendor   **f.** touring

1. During the summer, many _____ visit the United States.

2. Each traveler needs to bring a _____ in order to enter the country.

3. In New York City, the streets are usually _____ with people.

4. Many of the people are tourists going _____.

5. On some streets, they can buy hot dogs and other snacks from a _____.

6. In America, it is the _____ to shake hands with people you meet.

Name _____

Character Chart

Yunmi's Feelings	Story Clues
About Her Visit to Korea excited anxious	*(See page 145.)*
About Her Korean Cousins jealous	*(See pages 150–153 and 158–160.)* They take her sightseeing.
About Halmoni ashamed about being selfish	*(See pages 152–153 and 157–159.)*

What do you think Yunmi will do if her cousins come to visit
her in New York? Explain why you think as you do.

_____

_____

Name _____

Finish the Letter

Suppose Yunmi wrote this letter. Write story details to finish her letter.

Dear Anna Marie,

We've had a wonderful time in Korea! When

_____ and I first arrived

at the airport, I had to stand in the line for

_____. That made me feel

strange. However, my Korean family made me feel welcome.

I loved sightseeing and shopping, and my cousins Jinhi and

Sunhi helped me _____. For a

time I became sad, because I thought that my grandmother

_____. Then we went to my

grandfather's gravesite to _____.

That's where Halmoni told me that she would be

_____.

Next year I hope that my cousins will come to New York

for a visit. You can help me take them sightseeing! I'll be

home soon, and I can't wait to see you.

Your friend,

Yunmi

Name _____

Other Outcomes

Read the story. Then complete the chart on the next page.

Ando's Journey

Long ago in Japan, Ando loved to draw. He knew that one day he must follow in his father's footsteps. He must become head firefighter at the castle, as was the custom. But Ando loved to draw.

When Ando was twelve, his mother died. The next year, his father died, so Ando started to work. But he missed drawing so much that he set out to find a teacher. He had to study art.

Ando's first choice was a very famous artist. He begged the artist to help him, but the man simply turned him down, as did many others. Finally, Ando found Toyohiro, a quiet artist who loved nature and made woodblock prints. Ando learned to love nature and make prints much as his teacher did. Ando's work was so beautiful that he helped make this new art style popular.

One day, Ando left for a long journey through Japan. He began drawing everything he saw — mountains, water, the boats in the harbor, people flying kites or drinking tea. Then he turned his pictures into woodblock prints. More than fifty years later, artists in Europe saw a collection of his works. The prints gave them new ideas on drawing and painting.

Name _____

Other Outcomes continued

**Answer each question by predicting an outcome.
Then give reasons why you think as you do.**

1. What if Ando's parents had not died when he was young?

Predicted Outcome

_____

Reasons

_____

_____

2. What if Ando had never found Toyohiro?

Predicted Outcome

_____

Reasons

_____

_____

3. What would have been the outcome if Ando had liked to
   stay home instead of travel?

Predicted Outcome

_____

Reasons

_____

_____

Name _____

Who Owns It?

▶ Add an **apostrophe** and *s* (*'s*) to a singular noun to make it show ownership. Add an **apostrophe** (*'*) to a plural noun that already ends with *s* to make it show ownership.

Halmoni**'s** hand   parents**'** names

Complete each sentence. Add an apostrophe and *s* or just an apostrophe to make each noun in dark type show ownership. The first one is done for you.

Last weekend, my family went to visit my (**mother**) _____mother's_____

sister. (**Aunt Jenny**) _____ house is

three hours away. I carried my two little (**sisters**) _____

bags out to the car. I couldn't lift my (**parents**) _____

suitcases because they were too heavy.

I was very excited to see my cousins. My (**cousins**) _____

names are Ryan and Marie. As soon as my family got there, Ryan and

Marie took me to their pet (**rabbits**) _____ cages

behind the house. (**Ryan**) _____ rabbit is named

Flopsy. (**Flopsy**) _____ ears hang straight down.

(**Marie**) _____ rabbit is named Topsy. (**Topsy**)

_____ ears stick straight up.

This time there was a surprise — a rabbit for me! My new (**rabbit**)

_____ name is Mopsy.

Name _____

The Vowel Sound in *bought*

When you hear the /ô/ sound, remember that it can be spelled with the pattern *ough* or *augh*.

/ô/ b**ough**t, c**augh**t

▶ In the starred words *laugh*, *through*, *enough*, and *cough*, the *ough* and *augh* patterns spell other sounds.

Write each Spelling Word under its *ough* or *augh* spelling pattern.

ough

_____ _____

_____ _____

_____ _____

augh

_____ _____

_____ _____

Spelling Spree

Only Opposites Write the Spelling Word that is the opposite of each clue.

1. caught
2. thought
3. bought
4. laugh*
5. through*
6. enough*
7. fought
8. daughter
9. taught
10. brought
11. ought
12. cough*

1. not sold, but _____

2. not learned, but _____

3. not dropped, but _____

4. not took, but _____

5. not son, but _____

6. not cry, but _____

Alphabet Puzzler Write the Spelling Word that goes in ABC order between each pair of words.

7. cool, _____, daze   7. _____

8. open, _____, paste   8. _____

9. thin, _____, thunder   9. _____

10. find, _____, game   10. _____

Proofreading and Writing

Proofreading Suppose Yunmi sent this note. Circle the five misspelled Spelling Words in it. Then write each word correctly.

Dear Mom and Dad,

    Halmoni and I are here in Korea! I thoght the plane ride was really neat. Everyone loves the presents we brought. We went throogh a palace today. I hope we have enouf time to see everything. Halmoni has baught some gifts for you. You will laugh when you see them!

        Your loving dauter,

        Yunmi

Spelling Words

1. caught
2. thought
3. bought
4. laugh*
5. through*
6. enough*
7. fought
8. daughter
9. taught
10. brought
11. ought
12. cough*

1. _____   4. _____

2. _____   5. _____

3. _____

✏️ **Write an Opinion** An **opinion** tells what you believe or feel about something. Think of two places you have visited. Did you like one place better than the other? Why?

On a separate sheet of paper, write an opinion. Tell about the places you visited, and explain why you liked one place better than the other. Use Spelling Words from the list.

Name _____

Everything in Its Place

**Read the first pair of words in each analogy below. Decide
how the words are related. Then write the word that best
completes the analogy.**

1. **Author** is to **book** as **painter** is to _____ .
   brush   picture   artist

2. **Breakfast** is to **dinner** as **morning** is to _____ .
   sun   toast   evening

3. **Scissors** is to **cut** as **pencil** is to _____ .
   write   yellow   crayon

4. **Twelve** is to **number** as **green** is to _____ .
   grass   color   shape

5. **Bee** is to **honey** as **hen** is to _____ .
   egg   corn   farm

6. **Rude** is to **polite** as **dishonest** is to _____ .
   calm   mean   honest

7. **Television** is to **watch** as **radio** is to _____ .
   listen   screen   volume

8. **Frog** is to **tadpole** as **butterfly** is to _____ .
   pretty   caterpillar   flying

 =   =

Name _____

Circling Object Pronouns

Circle each object pronoun in the paragraph below. Then write the object pronouns on the lines below the paragraph.

Sunhi shows Yunmi how to make dumplings. She gives her a thin dumpling skin and some filling. Yunmi rolls it. She places the new dumpling on a tray with the other dumplings. The girls take them to the picnic. They share the dumplings with us. Yunmi gives one to me to taste.

1. _____   4. _____

2. _____   5. _____

3. _____

Choose the correct word or phrase in parentheses to complete each sentence.

6. The picnic is a special event for

   _____. (we, us)

7. Yunmi tells _____ about life in New York. (they, them)

8. Halmoni tells _____ a story. (her, she)

9. Her voice makes _____ feel better. (me, I)

10. The picnic made _____ very
    happy. (me and Halmoni, Halmoni and me)

Rewriting with Object Pronouns

Object Pronouns	
Singular	**Plural**
me you him, her, it	us you them

Rewrite each sentence. Replace each underlined word or phrase with an object pronoun.

1. The airplane takes <u>Halmoni and Yunmi</u> to Korea.

   _____

2. Yunmi shows her passport to <u>the man</u>.

   _____

3. Outside the airport, Yunmi hugs <u>her cousins</u>.

   _____

4. Yunmi buys <u>the purse</u> for <u>Helen</u>.

   _____

5. Halmoni takes <u>Yunmi and her cousins</u> to the National Museum.

   _____

Name _____

Using the Correct Pronoun

What if Yunmi sent her friend this postcard? Circle any pronouns that are used incorrectly. Then rewrite the postcard.

Dear Helen,

Korea is wonderful. Halmoni and me arrived last week. Her showed me many wonderful sights. Us went to the National Museum with my cousins, Sunhi and Jinhi. Them took us to a market too. One vendor sold bean cakes. Sunhi and I picked out this card.

Halmoni showed I and Sunhi how to make dumplings. I will be home soon. Me and you will make some dumplings!

Bye,
Yunmi

_____

_____

_____

_____

_____

_____

_____

_____

Name _____

Writing a Message

Use this page to take a message.

Date: _____ Time: _____

For: _____

From: _____ Telephone number: _____

Message: _____

_____

_____

_____

_____

_____

_____

Message taken by: _____

Name _____

Using Complete Information

Suppose Yunmi and Halmoni each made a phone call. "Listen" to each answering machine and read the message. Make the messages complete by adding any missing information.

1. Hi, Halmoni, it's Yunmi. It's 3:00 on Monday. Junhi and I are going to the park. We will be home at 5:30. If you need us, you can call Mr. Choi's market at 333-6748. He will get the message to us.

Day: Monday. **Time:** _____
For: Halmoni
Caller: _____
Caller's number: _____
Message: Junhi and I are going to the _____ . We will be home at _____ . Call Mr. Choi's market if you need us.

2. Hello, Junhi and Sunhi. This is Halmoni, on Tuesday at 11:30. I want you to teach Yunmi how to make mandoo on Wednesday afternoon. I'll be home to help you. Leave a message for me at 333-2135.

Day: _____ **Time:** 11:30
For: Junhi _____
Caller: Halmoni
Caller's number: 333-2135
Message: Teach Yunmi how to make mandoo _____
_____ I'll be home to help you. Leave a message for me at _____ .

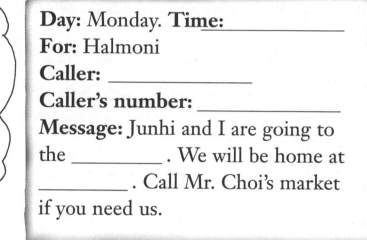

Name _____

Selection Vocabulary

Cross out the word that doesn't belong.

1. terrain   earth   sky   land

2. grueling   resting   tiring   difficult

3. perilous   dangerous   safe   risky

4. deserted   empty   uninhabited   bustling

True or False?

5. It is easy to walk across something <u>impassable</u>.

   _____

6. Ice sheets floating on water are called <u>floes</u>.

   _____

7. Land that is <u>barren</u> has many plants and animals.

   _____

8. A <u>crevasse</u> is a deep crack.

   _____

Name _____

Text Organization Chart

Text Feature	Where It Is	Purpose
heading (date)		
photograph, caption, illustration		
definition		
chronological sequence		

Shackleton Survives!

**Complete the news report by
adding the missing information.**

Sir Ernest Shackleton and his crew survived many hardships on

their recent voyage to _____. Hundreds

of miles from land, their ship, the _____,

became _____. The men camped for

months on slowly moving _____. When they

reached open water, they set out in lifeboats on a perilous voyage to

_____.

There, the men split up. Shackleton and five others sailed on

toward _____. The

six men finally landed. Shackleton and two others hiked across tall

_____ to get to a _____,

where they hoped to find _____.

On May 20, 1916, the three exhausted men reached safety, but the

voyage did not really end until more than three months later, when

Shackleton _____

_____.

Name _____

Organized Hike

**Read this news story. Then complete the chart
on the next page.**

Hiker Stranded

Lost

7:00 P.M. on April 1: Donald McCarthy, 53, of Keene,
New Hampshire, got lost while hiking along an old logging
trail near Waterville Valley. (A logging trail is used by workers
who take away cut trees.) By nightfall, McCarthy knew he
would have to spend the night in the woods.

. . . and Found

8:00 P.M.: A Fish and Game officer thought he spotted
McCarthy and called out. McCarthy never answered, and the
officer moved on. The next morning, McCarthy was found.
When questioned by Fish and Game, McCarthy admitted he
thought he heard someone call, but he also heard noises in the
brush. "I was sure it was a bear," McCarthy said, "so I kept
quiet and climbed into a tree for the night."

**This sign led McCarthy
into thinking he heard bears.**

Organized Hike   continued

Finish the chart with text features from "Hiker Stranded." Explain the purpose of each feature.

Example of Text Feature	Purpose of the Text Feature
Heading _____ _____	_____ _____
Caption _____ _____	_____ _____
Definition _____ _____	_____ _____
Chronological sequence (dates, times) _____ _____	_____ _____

If you were a reporter, what other information would you add?
What text feature would you use to give more information?

_____

_____

Name _____

VCCV Challenge

**Write the VCCV word that matches each clue in the puzzle.
Use the Word Bank and a dictionary for help.**

Across

1. soaking wet
6. wood used for building
7. the coldest season
8. captain of a ship
9. to save from danger

Down

1. the peak of a mountain
2. cloth used for making tents or sails
3. an Antarctic bird
4. a long trip
5. to remain alive

---

canvas	lumber	penguin	soggy	skipper
journey	winter	rescue	survive	summit

Name _____

The VCCV Pattern

To spell a word with the VCCV pattern, divide the word between the two consonants. Look for spelling patterns you have learned. Spell the word by syllables.

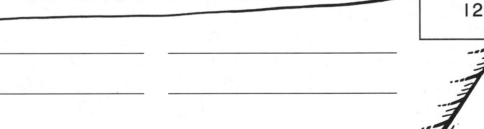

vc|cv

Mon | day

vc|cv

sud | den

Write each Spelling Word under the head that tells where the word is divided into syllables.

Spelling Words

1. Monday
2. sudden
3. until
4. forget
5. happen
6. follow
7. dollar
8. window
9. hello
10. market
11. pretty
12. order

Between Different Consonants

_____   _____

_____   _____

_____

Between Double Consonants

_____   _____

_____   _____

_____

Spelling Spree

Silly Statements   Each statement was made by a South Pole visitor. Write the Spelling Word that best completes each sentence.

1. I will not sell my mittens for a _____.

2. I won't go home _____ I've seen a whale.

3. A seal just tried to climb through my _____.

4. I said _____ to the iceberg as it passed.

5. Please run to the _____ to buy some oranges.

6. That polar bear keeps trying to _____ me around.

7. The little bird in the tux will take your _____.

1. _____
2. _____
3. _____
4. _____
5. _____
6. _____
7. _____

Proofreading and Writing

Proofreading Circle the five misspelled Spelling Words in this script. Then write each word correctly.

Sam: We are leaving Mondy for a trip to the South Pole.

Emma: Wow! I didn't know that. Is this a suddin trip?

Sam: No, we've been planning it for ages. I hear it's a really pritty place.

Emma: If you hapen to see any penguins, say hello for me.

Sam: Sure. If you want me to say hi to a killer whale, though, you can ferget it!

Spelling Words

1. Monday
2. sudden
3. until
4. forget
5. happen
6. follow
7. dollar
8. window
9. hello
10. market
11. pretty
12. order

1. _____

2. _____

3. _____

4. _____

5. _____

Write a List How would you prepare for a trip to the South Pole? Would you need to buy things? If so, what? Where would you buy the goods?

On a separate sheet of paper, write a list of things to do to get ready for a trip to the South Pole. Use Spelling Words from the list.

Name _____

Sounds the Same

From the word box below, choose a pair of homophones to complete each pair of sentences. Choose the spelling that fits the meaning of the sentence and write it in the blank. Use a dictionary if you are not sure which is which.

not	one	see	threw	bear
knot	won	sea	through	bare

1. a. I stood on the ship's deck and looked out at the

   _____.

   b. I could _____ nothing but water and sky.

2. a. Jen _____ the ball.

   b. It went _____ the hoop!

3. a. There was a _____ in Jeb's shoelace.

   b. He could _____ untie it.

4. a. The _____ ground was now covered with

   snow.

   b. The big _____ left tracks where he walked.

5. a. Our team has only _____ good pitcher.

   b. Even so, we have _____ every game.

Name _____

Writing Possessively

Write the possessive pronoun in each sentence.

1. The men began their voyage in 1915. _____

2. Shackleton and his crew were very brave. _____

3. Our class read about the amazing adventure. _____

4. I asked my teacher about ice floes. _____

5. Her explanation was clear and helpful. _____

Write the possessive pronoun that could take the place of the underlined word or words.

6. I think that Shackleton's story is remarkable. _____

7. I admire the men's courage. _____

8. The station's light was a marvelous sight. _____

9. Shackleton returned to John, Chippy, and Tim's camp.

_____

10. Thoralf was happy to see Thoralf's old friend.

_____

Name _____

Choosing Possessives

**Choose the correct word in parentheses to complete
each sentence.**

1. Shackleton led _____ crew to Antarctica. (him, his)

2. The *Endurance* was a useless hulk, lying on _____ side. (it's, its)

3. The men carried _____ food with them. (they, their)

4. _____ journey was just beginning. (Their, There)

5. Shackleton described _____ plan. (he's, his)

6. The lifeboats were _____ only hope. (their, they're)

7. Each boat had _____ own sled. (its, its')

8. _____ class studied the perilous trip. (Our, Ours)

9. I decided to write _____ story about Antarctica. (me, my)

10. Is _____ story about Shackleton? (your, you)

Name _____

Writing a Story

Alana wrote a story about Shackleton's crew. Proofread Alana's writing. Check that *its* and *it's* are used correctly. Then rewrite the letter on the lines below.

May 19, 1916

Its very cold again today. John and Chippy are still very ill. The sun is bright, but it's light brings no heat. This barren land is deserted and lonely.

I explored the terrain yesterday. Its difficult to follow a trail. At last, I killed a seal. It's meat will feed us for several days. The food is so cold it has lost it's taste.

I hope that Shackleton and the others can survive their journey. Its hard to imagine a more grueling adventure.

_____

_____

_____

_____

_____

_____

_____

_____

Name _____

A Learning Log Entry

Pick two examples of your own writing. Carefully reread your work. Complete the Learning Log entry. List what you have learned under *What I Learned*. List what needs more work under *My Goals*.

LEARNING LOG	
Writing sample 1: _____	Date: _____
Writing sample 2: _____	Date: _____

What I Learned:	**My Goals:**
_____	_____
_____	_____
_____	_____
_____	_____
_____	_____
_____	_____
_____	_____

Name _____

Using Dates and Times

▶ Dates are written: Month, day, year. A comma separates the day and year. Dates can also be written in numerals with slash marks.

> The fifth of February in 2003: February 5, 2003
> or 2/5/03

▶ A.M. stands for morning, from one minute after midnight until noon. Seven o'clock in the morning: 7:00 A.M.

▶ P.M. stands for after noon, from one minute after noon until midnight. Nine o'clock in the evening: 9:00 P.M.

Write each date two ways.

1. The seventh day of April in 2011

   _____   _____

2. The thirty-first of October in 2006

   _____   _____

Write each time.

3. Six-fifteen
   (after noon)

   _____

4. Eight thirty-five
   (morning)

   _____

5. Ten minutes after ten
   (morning)

   _____

6. Forty minutes after nine
   (after noon)

   _____

Name _____

Writing an Answer to a Question

Use what you have learned about taking tests to help you write answers to questions about something you have read. This practice will help you when you take this kind of test.

Read these paragraphs from the story *Yunmi and Halmoni's Trip*.

> Yunmi had only been to a cemetery once before. She had seen people place flowers at a grave, say a prayer, and leave quietly. But in Korea, no one cried or looked sad. The cousins ran through the field collecting flowers and smooth stones for Grandfather's hill.
>
> Yunmi wanted to talk with Halmoni, but everyone was crowded around her. Yunmi went and sat under a big tree all by herself to think. As she watched Halmoni, Yunmi grew more and more afraid that Halmoni would not want to go back to New York.

Now write your answer to each question.

1. How do you think Yunmi's life would change if her grandmother, Halmoni, did not go back to New York with her?

_____

_____

_____

_____

Name _____

Writing an Answer to
a Question continued

2. What does Yunmi do when she worries about going back to
New York without her grandmother?

_____

_____

_____

_____

3. How do people in Korea act when they visit a grave in a cemetery?

_____

_____

_____

_____

Name _____

Spelling Review

Write Spelling Words from the list on this page to answer the questions.

1–8. Which eight words have the vowel sound in **loose** or **look**?

1. _____   5. _____

2. _____   6. _____

3. _____   7. _____

4. _____   8. _____

9–15. Which seven words have the vowel sound in **fought**?

9. _____   13. _____

10. _____   14. _____

11. _____   15. _____

12. _____

16–26. Which eleven words have the VCCV pattern?
Hint: You have already written one of these words.

16. _____   22. _____

17. _____   23. _____

18. _____   24. _____

19. _____   25. _____

20. _____   26. _____

21. _____

Spelling Words

1. bought
2. order
3. grew
4. hello
5. thought
6. happen
7. forget
8. caught
9. flew
10. spoon
11. daughter
12. window
13. dollar
14. brought
15. cook
16. boot
17. Monday
18. sudden
19. pretty
20. until
21. ought
22. balloon
23. chew
24. taught
25. tooth

Name _____

Spelling Spree

New TV Shows! Write the Spelling Word that best completes each title of a new TV show. Remember to use capital letters.

1. *Sook Can _____, Bake, and Roast*
2. *Look Out the _____. What Do You See?*
3. *The Superhero Who _____ Too High*
4. *Alphabetical _____: A Game Show for the Very Young*
5. *I _____ to Have Brought My Camera*
6. *A _____ Storm Springs Up in Egypt*
7. *Always _____ Your Food Well*
8. *Tongue, _____, and Throat: Have a Healthy Mouth*

1. _____   5. _____

2. _____   6. _____

3. _____   7. _____

4. _____   8. _____

A Strange Hike A few words are missing from this paragraph. Use a Spelling Word to fill in each blank.

We went hiking on 9. _____. It had to

10. _____ that the laces on my left

11. _____ broke. Then we found out that no

one had 12. _____ any food. However, we did

find one plastic 13. _____. The weather was warm

14. _____ the afternoon. That's when we went home.

Name _____

Proofreading and Writing

Proofreading Circle the five misspelled Spelling
Words below. Then write each word correctly.

1. balloon
2. thought
3. grew
4. caught
5. forget
6. bought
7. pretty
8. dollar
9. until
10. taught
11. daughter
12. hello

I flew in a hot-air baloon! My uncle bot it from
his friend. I never thoght it could go so high. The city
looked pritty from up high. I will never fourget the ride.

1. _____   4. _____

2. _____   5. _____

3. _____

Today's News Fix this speech. Write the Spelling
Word that is the opposite of each underlined word.

Who 6. <u>learned</u> that we all should travel by car? Last year,
the number of cars 7. <u>shrank</u>. Even my 8. <u>son</u> has her own car.
Say good-bye to cars and 9. <u>good-bye</u> to trains! People have
10. <u>let go</u> of the excitement of train travel. If everyone gave one
11. <u>coin</u>, we could have a train tomorrow, but 12. <u>after</u> then, we
won't!

6. _____   9. _____   12. _____

7. _____   10. _____

8. _____   11. _____

✏ **Write a Story** On another sheet of paper, write
about a trip you would like to take. Use the Spelling
Review Words.

Name _____

Best Beginnings

Write a shorter version of the opening sentences of each biography. Then describe which opening most made you want to read the rest of the biography.

Becoming a Champion: The Babe Didrikson Story

_____

_____

Bill Meléndez: An Artist in Motion

_____

_____

Brave Bessie Coleman: Pioneer Aviator

_____

_____

Hank Greenberg: All-Around All-Star

_____

_____

Which opening made you want to read the biography?

_____

How might reading this biography change your life?

_____

Name _____

When They Were Young

Write one fact about each person's childhood. Tell how that fact affected each person as an adult.

Babe Didrikson

_____

_____

Bill Meléndez

_____

_____

Bessie Coleman

_____

_____

Hank Greenberg

_____

_____

What is something you can do as a young person that will help you when you are grown-up?

_____

_____

Name _____

Smart Solutions

**Describe a problem that you would like to solve.
Tell why you think it is important to solve it.**

_____

_____

_____

_____

_____

_____

_____

What could you do to help solve this problem?

_____

_____

_____

_____

_____

Name _____

Smart Solutions

Fill in the chart as you read the stories.

	Pepita Talks Twice	Poppa's New Pants	Ramona Quimby, Age 8
What is the problem?			
How is the problem solved?			

Name _____

Create a Crossword!

Use the words in the box to create your own crossword puzzle. On another sheet of paper, write a clue for each word you use.

Vocabulary

enchiladas	language	Spanish	salsa
tacos	tamales	tortilla	

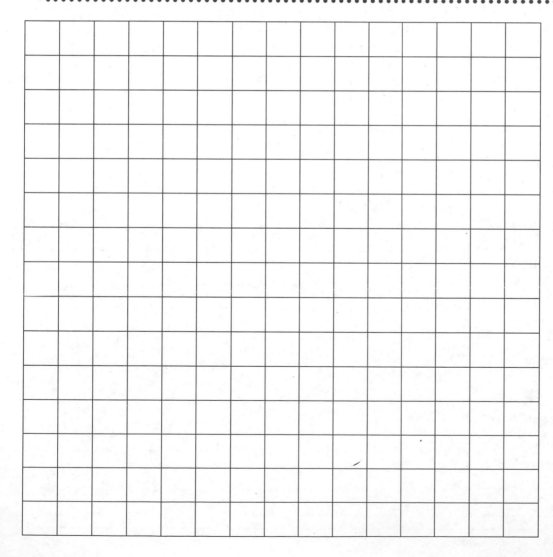

Name _____

Problem-Solving Chart

Problem: Pepita does not like having to talk twice.

Possible Solutions	Pros (+) and Cons (−)
1. Stop speaking Spanish.	(+) You wouldn't have to talk twice for people anymore. (−) _____ _____
2. Stop speaking English.	(+) _____ _____ (−) _____ _____
3. Get mad and point out that you don't have time to speak twice.	(+) _____ _____ (−) _____ _____
4. Politely say that you can't speak twice when you don't have time.	(+) _____ _____ (+) _____ _____

Name _____

What Happened?

**Mark a T if the sentence is true and an F if it is false.
If the sentence is false, rewrite it to make it correct.**

1. Pepita's dog is a wolf.

   _____

2. Some adults in Pepita's neighborhood speak only Spanish.

   _____

3. Pepita loses her temper when Juan gets home first and teaches
   Lobo to fetch a ball.

   _____

4. Before she makes her decision, Pepita thinks about all the
   problems she might have if she stops speaking Spanish.

   _____

5. Lobo does not understand Pepita when she speaks in English.

   _____

6. Pepita's father is happy when he learns that Pepita has stopped speaking
   Spanish.

   _____

Write a complete sentence to answer the question below.

What event finally convinces Pepita that it is a good thing to
speak both English and Spanish?

_____

Name _____

A Homework Problem

Read the story. Then complete the chart on the next page.

The Volcano or Numberland

"Pakki! Help me in the kitchen! Now! Hurry!" I ran down
to the kitchen, terrified. There sat my sister, Kayla, drinking
milk and calmly reading the television listings in the newspaper.

"What's wrong?" I asked, out of breath from running to
the kitchen.

"The science project I've been working on for two weeks
is due tomorrow. Ms. Odenpak may give me a bad grade if I
don't have my model volcano finished. But a TV show called
Niles in Numberland is starting in twenty minutes. My math
teacher, Mr. Browning, told us to watch it and be ready to talk
about it tomorrow in class. What I should do? Help!"

"I have three ideas," I answered. "One, you finish your
volcano while I watch the TV show and
take notes. Of course, I'm not very good
at taking notes," I reminded her. "Two,
you can watch the TV show and ask Ms.
Odenpak for an extra day to finish your
volcano. Or three, you can work on
your volcano in front of the television
while you take notes on the show."

"Hmm," Kayla answered, thinking
deeply. "Which one's the best solution?"

Name _____

A Homework Problem continued

**Read the problem. Write one possible solution from the story
in each box. Then give a pro and a con about the solution.**

The Problem: Kayla needs to finish her science project, and
she also needs to watch TV for a math assignment.

Possible Solution: _____

_____

Pro: _____

Con: _____

Possible Solution: _____

_____

Pro: _____

Con: _____

Possible Solution: _____

_____

Pro: _____

Con: _____

Which of these solutions do you think is the best? Why?

_____

Name _____

Playing with the Pattern

Read each word in dark type. Then follow the directions to make a new word. Write the new word on the line, and draw a picture in the box to show its meaning.

Example: single   Replace si with ju.

The new word is _____jungle_____.

1. **bundle**   Replace **bu** with **ca**.

   The new word is _____.

2. **dollar**   Replace **lar** with **phin**.

   The new word is _____.

3. **twinkle**   Replace **twi** with **a**.

   The new word is _____.

4. **letter**   Replace **let** with **mons**.

   The new word is _____.

5. **turtle**   Replace **tur** with **cas**.

   The new word is _____.

Name _____

Words That End with *er* or *le*

Spelling Words

1. summer
2. winter
3. little
4. October
5. travel*
6. color*
7. apple
8. able
9. November
10. ever
11. later
12. purple

Remember that, in words with more than one syllable,
the final /ər/ sounds are often spelled *er*; and
the final /əl/ sounds can be spelled *le*.

/ər/ summ**er**   /əl/ litt**le**

► In the starred word *travel*, the /əl/ sound is spelled *el*.
► In the starred word *color*, the /ər/ sound is spelled *or*.

**Write each Spelling Word under the heading that
describes the word.**

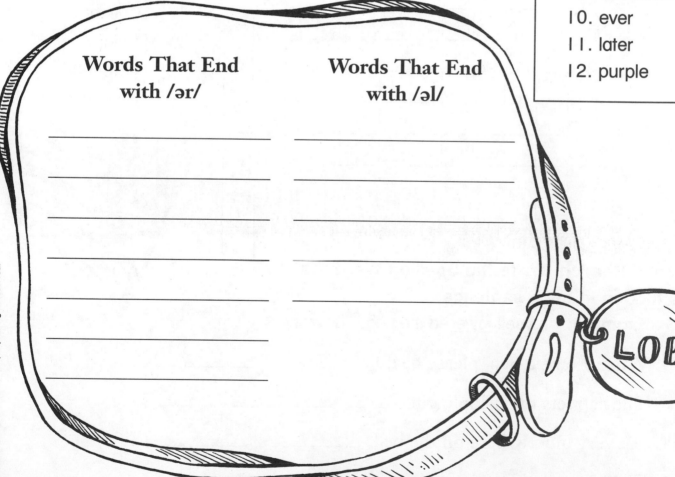

**Words That End
with /ər/**

**Words That End
with /əl/**

Name _____

Spelling Spree

Crossword Puzzle **Write a Spelling Word in the puzzle that means the same as each clue.**

Across

3. the month before December
4. not big
6. the month after September
7. red or yellow or green

Down

1. the hottest season
2. take a trip
4. the opposite of *sooner*
5. a mix of blue and red

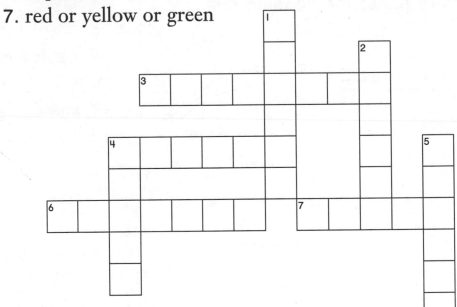

Word Search **Write the Spelling Word that is hidden in each sentence.**

Example: I myse<u>lf lowe</u>red the flag.   **flower**

9. When I take a nap, please be quiet. _____

10. The cab lets two people out. _____

11. Lie very quietly here on the bed. _____

12. We'll win terrific prizes! _____

Proofreading and Writing

Proofreading Circle the five misspelled Spelling Words in this paragraph. Then write each word correctly.

Sarah liked summir. It was her favorite time of year. The heat did not evir bother her. Her parents, however, did not like the heat. They often wished to travil someplace cool. When Sarah got hot, she rested in the cool kitchen. Later, she would eat a nice, juicy appel. She liked the fruit's pleasant red coler and smooth skin. It was too bad her parents weren't able to enjoy this season as much as she did.

Spelling Words

1. summer
2. winter
3. little
4. October
5. travel*
6. color*
7. apple
8. able
9. November
10. ever
11. later
12. purple

1. _____   4. _____

2. _____   5. _____

3. _____

Write a Paragraph What can Sarah do to help her parents stay cool? How can Sarah get her parents to like the summer as much as she does?

On a separate sheet of paper, write a paragraph about what Sarah might do or say to her parents to help them enjoy the summer. Use Spelling Words from the list.

Name _____

In Other Words

Choose a synonym for each word from the word box below. Write the synonym in the blanks next to the word. Then write each numbered letter in the matching blanks to solve the puzzle.

Word Bank

| foolish | loud | stroll | tugged | yell |
| frighten | speed | tired | wealth | |

1. walk   ___ ___ ___ ___ ___ ___
               1

2. shout   ___ ___ ___ ___
               3

3. pulled   ___ ___ ___ ___ ___ ___
               6

4. scare   ___ ___ ___ ___ ___ ___ ___ ___
                         2

5. sleepy   ___ ___ ___ ___ ___
               7

6. race   ___ ___ ___ ___ ___
            4

7. riches   ___ ___ ___ ___ ___ ___
               5

8. noisy   ___ ___ ___ ___
               8

9. silly   ___ ___ ___ ___ ___ ___ ___
                              9

This is a word for a book of synonyms:

___ ___ ___ ___ ___ ___ ___ ___ ___
 1   2   3   4   5   6   7   8   9

Name _____

Writing with Adjectives

On the lines to the right of each sentence, list the adjectives. Then write each adjective in the chart below.

1. Pepita has one playful dog. _____

2. She has many friendly neighbors. _____

3. Pepita has an unusual problem. _____

4. She speaks perfect Spanish and English. _____

5. She does not confuse the two languages. _____

6. Pepita gets an angry feeling. _____

7. Juan teaches Lobo a new trick. _____

8. Mother makes a dozen tacos. _____

9. She also prepares some salsa. _____

10. Pepita learns an important lesson. _____

What Kind?	**How Many?**	**Articles**
_____	_____	_____
_____	_____	_____
_____	_____	_____
_____	_____	
_____		
_____		

Theme 6: **Smart Solutions** 131

Name _____

Adjectives in Paragraphs

**Read this paragraph about a neighborhood.
Choose an adjective from the box to complete each
sentence. Use the clues in parentheses to help you.**

Word Bank

an	beautiful	exciting	favorite	full
happy	hundred	long	several	the

Carlos's neighborhood has an _____

(what kind) block party. Almost a _____

(how many) people are there. Many people help to prepare

_____(article) excellent meal. Two _____

(what kind) tables are covered with _____

(what kind) plates. Carlos and _____

(how many) neighbors sing their _____

(what kind) songs. The _____ (what

kind) words are in Spanish. Soon, everyone joins _____

(article) singers. Even the dog woofs a _____

(what kind) bark at the end of every song.

Name _____

Expanding Sentences with Adjectives

Rewrite each sentence. Add at least one adjective to each sentence. Remember that you may need to change *a* or *an*, too.

1. Pepita and Juan have a dog.

_____

2. Pepita goes to a picnic.

_____

3. She helps prepare the food.

_____

4. The neighbors sing songs.

_____

5. Lobo almost runs into a truck.

_____

6. Pepita calls the dog.

_____

7. The dog hears her shout.

_____

8. She gives Lobo a hug.

_____

Name _____

Announcement Planner

**Use this page to organize your ideas for an
announcement. Write an announcement about a birth,
wedding, concert, fair, parade, or other special event.**

Who?	What?	Where?	When?	Why?	How?

ANNOUNCEMENT

_____

_____

_____

_____

_____

_____

_____

Name _____

Ordering Important Information

► When writing an announcement, first decide what information is most important. Put that information first.
► Put other information in order of importance from most important to least important.
► Be sure your announcement includes all the necessary information that answers some or all of these questions: Who? What? Where? When? How? Why?

Number the information in the order it should go in the announcement. Write 1 for the first thing that should be in the announcement. Write 2 for the second thing.

_____ Practice will be at Jamal's house.

_____ Practice will end at noon.

_____ There will be band practice on Saturday.

_____ Practice begins at 10:00 a.m.

_____ Jamal's address is 32 Windsor Lane.

Rewrite the announcement in the order you marked.

_____

_____

_____

_____

_____

Name _____

Revising Your Essay

Reread your persuasive essay. What do you need to make it better? Use this page to help you decide. Put a checkmark in the box for each sentence that describes your persuasive essay.

Rings the Bell!

☐ My essay has an attention-grabbing beginning.

☐ I state my goal clearly and give reasons to support it.

☐ I use facts and examples to support my opinion.

☐ The essay is interesting to read and convincing.

Getting Stronger

☐ I could make the beginning more attention grabbing.

☐ I state my goal, but could add reasons to support it.

☐ I need more facts and examples to make it convincing.

☐ There are some run-on sentences I need to fix.

☐ There are a few other mistakes.

Try Harder

☐ I need a better beginning.

☐ I don't state my goals or reasons for my opinion.

☐ I need to add facts and examples.

☐ This isn't very convincing.

☐ There are a lot of mistakes.

Name _____

Correcting Run-On Sentences

Fix these run-on sentences. Write the sentences correctly on the lines provided.

1. <u>Run-On</u>: Jane Goodall is one of the world's great scientists, she studies chimpanzees.

   <u>Corrected</u>: _____

   _____

2. <u>Run-On</u>: More than thirty years ago Goodall had an interesting idea, she would study chimps in their natural habitat.

   <u>Corrected</u>: _____

   _____

3. <u>Run-On</u>: At first, the chimps were suspicious, gradually Goodall gained their trust.

   <u>Corrected</u>: _____

   _____

4. <u>Run-On</u>: Goodall got to know each chimp in the group, each chimp was given a name.

   <u>Corrected</u>: _____

   _____

5. <u>Run-On</u>: Goodall was the first to discover that chimps made tools, she also discovered that chimps could learn new ideas.

   <u>Corrected</u>: _____

   _____

Name _____

Spelling Words

Look for spelling patterns you have learned to help you remember the Spelling Words on this page. Think about the parts that you find hard to spell.

Write the missing letters and apostrophes in the Spelling Words below.

1. h ____ ____

2. I ____ ____

3. I ____ ____

4. th ____ ____ ____ ____

5. did ____ ____ ____

6. do ____ ____ ____

7. ____ ' ____ ow

8. ____ ____ tsid ____

9. b ____ ____ n

10. we ____ ____ ____

11. ____ nyone

12. ____ nyway

Spelling Words

1. his
2. I'd
3. I'm
4. that's
5. didn't
6. don't
7. know
8. outside
9. been
10. we're
11. anyone
12. anyway

Study List On another sheet of paper, write each Spelling Word. Check the list to be sure you spelled each word correctly.

Name _____

Spelling Spree

Contraction Math Add the first word to the second word to get a contraction from the Spelling Word list.

1. do + not = _____   1. _____

2. we + are = _____   2. _____

3. that + is = _____   3. _____

4. I + had = _____   4. _____

5. did + not = _____   5. _____

6. I + am = _____   6. _____

Fill in the Blanks Fill each blank in these sentences with the Spelling Word that makes the most sense.

It's freezing __7__ ! Has __8__ seen my jacket? I've __9__ keeping it on the floor in my room, but it's not there. Now I don't __10__ where it is. Dad said it's not in __11__ study, either. Well __12__, if you see it, let me know.

7. _____   10. _____

8. _____   11. _____

9. _____   12. _____

Spelling Words

1. his
2. I'd
3. I'm
4. that's
5. didn't
6. don't
7. know
8. outside
9. been
10. we're
11. anyone
12. anyway

Name _____

Proofreading and Writing

Proofreading Circle the four misspelled Spelling
Words in this advertisement. Then write each word
correctly.

Do you have a problem that you don't kno

how to solve? Then call us at Smart

Solutions! We've bin solving people's

problems for over twenty years. And anywon

will tell you that our prices can't be beat. So

give us a call at 555-1971 — weare waiting!

Spelling Words

1. his
2. I'd
3. I'm
4. that's
5. didn't
6. don't
7. know
8. outside
9. been
10. we're
11. anyone
12. anyway

1. _____   3. _____

2. _____   4. _____

Write a Caption Draw a picture of a problem that needs to
be solved. Then write a caption describing the problem and
how to fix it. Use Spelling Words from the list.

Name _____

Sewing Words

Fill in the blanks with the correct word from the Word Bank. (Hint: Not every word will be used.) Then find and circle all the Word Bank words in the puzzle.

Word Bank

fabric	hem	mended	pattern
rustling	plaid	draped	

1. Another word for cloth is _____.

2. To make pants shorter, you could _____ them.

3. A shirt with a hole in it needs to be _____.

4. Different-colored stripes that cross one another make a

   design called _____.

5. If you are wearing a shirt with a decorative design on it, the

   shirt has a _____.

```
C R R D R A P E D M Q Y S
F L U B F D A S O G M R E
O T S N A C T T M J P E D
H Q T U B B T Y E G L U C
E M L N R J E M N Y A A A
M C I W I J R P D N I S O
Z U N V C H N S E O D S Z
K E G B Q T W G D W U O I
H E Q E B Y Q J E F P R J
```

Conclusions Chart

Pages	Questions
284–286	1. What is the narrator's name? _____ Which story clues helped you? _____ _____
286	2. How does Poppa feel about plaid pants? Which story clues helped you? _____ _____
288	3. How does George feel about being kissed by Big Mama and Aunt Viney? _____ Which story clues helped you? _____ _____
292	4. Who is the first shape? _____ Which story clues helped you? _____

Name _____

Who, What, and Why?

**Use complete sentences to answer the questions about
Poppa's New Pants.**

Who comes to visit Grandma Tiny, Poppa, and George?

_____

What is wrong with the pants Poppa buys?

_____

Why won't the women hem Poppa's pants?

_____

Why does George have trouble getting to sleep?

_____

_____

What weird sights does George see?

_____

_____

What is Grandma Tiny's surprise?

_____

Why do the women surprise each other?

_____

_____

Why does George feel lucky about the mix-up?

_____

_____

Theme 6: **Smart Solutions**   143

Name _____

Drawing Conclusions

Read the story. Then complete the chart on the next page.

The Pink Sweatshirt

"But Mom, I need a *pink* sweatshirt for our play!" I argued. "I'm the pig who builds with bricks! We need pink sweatshirts with hoods so we can sew on pink felt ears."

"Linda, I just bought you a white sweatshirt," said Mom. "You'll have to spend your own money if you want a pink one."

I was saving all my money for a new bike. "Oh, Mom! Tina's and Ali's parents are buying them pink ones," I whined.

This did not convince my mother. "Lots of pigs aren't pink," she said firmly. "You can be a white pig in a white sweatshirt."

But Tina, Ali, and I wanted our costumes to match. So, I got my new pair of red shorts, the ones labeled, "Wash in COLD WATER only." I dumped those and my white sweatshirt into the washing machine. Then I punched the button marked HOT WATER. Too bad I didn't look in the washer first! The load of white laundry left in there got washed again (in hot water) with my sweatshirt and red shorts.

So, today I'm spending my savings on new white socks for my brother, a white shirt for Dad, and four white towels. Luckily, Dad likes the new color of his bathrobe. It reminds him of a strawberry milkshake.

Name _____

Drawing Conclusions continued

Answer each question about "The Pink Sweatshirt." Then tell which story clues helped you to draw that conclusion.

1. Who is the girl telling the story?

_____

Story Clues: _____

_____

2. What happens when you wash red and white laundry together in hot water?

_____

Story Clues: _____

_____

_____

3. What other laundry was already in the washing machine?

_____

Story Clues: _____

_____

4. Why must Linda spend the money she is trying to save?

_____

Story Clues: _____

_____

Name _____

Which One Belongs?

Write the word from the box that belongs in each group.

Word Bank

cover	writer	below	finish	second
siren	female	frozen	shiver	clever

1. instant, moment, _____

2. under, beneath, _____

3. shake, tremble, _____

4. cold, icy, _____

5. smart, intelligent, _____

6. author, poet, _____

7. whistle, horn, _____

8. hide, cloak, _____

9. girl, woman, _____

10. end, complete, _____

146   Theme 6: **Smart Solutions**

Name _____

Words That Begin with *a* or *be*

In two-syllable words, the unstressed /ə/ sound at the beginning of a word may be spelled *a*. The unstressed /bĭ/ sounds may be spelled *be*.

/ə/ **a**gain   /bĭ/ **be**fore

Write each Spelling Word under the heading that tells how the word begins.

Spelling Words

1. began
2. again
3. around
4. before
5. away
6. about
7. alive
8. because
9. ahead
10. between
11. behind
12. ago

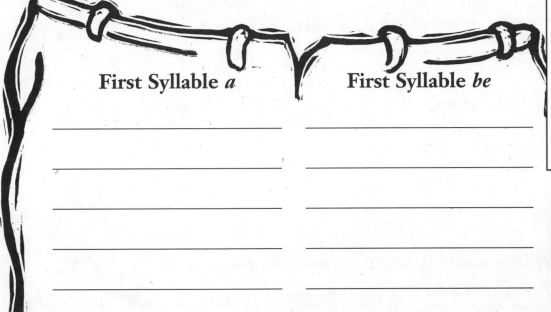

First Syllable *a*

_____

_____

_____

_____

_____

First Syllable *be*

_____

_____

_____

_____

_____

Name _____

Spelling Spree

Code Breaker Use the code to figure out each
Spelling Word below. Then write the word.

∞ = be   ^ = a   ⌐ = g

⊗ = n   ∇ = i   _ = o

Example: ∞ t w e e ⊗   _between_

1. ^ w ^ y   _____

2. ^ b _ u t   _____

3. ∞ h ∇ ⊗ d   _____

4. ∞ c ^ u s e   _____

5. ^ ⌐ ^ ∇ ⊗   _____

6. ^ r _ u ⊗ d   _____

7. ∞ f _ r e   _____

Rhyme Time Write a Spelling Word on each line
that rhymes with the name in the sentence.

Example: Where are _____, Faye? _they_

8. It's _____, Clive. _____

9. What's _____, Ned? _____

10. That was long _____, Joe. _____

11. We already _____, Jan. _____

12. Put them in _____, Jean. _____

Spelling Words

1. began
2. again
3. around
4. before
5. away
6. about
7. alive
8. because
9. ahead
10. between
11. behind
12. ago

Name _____

Proofreading and Writing

Proofreading Circle the five misspelled Spelling Words in this journal entry. Then write each word correctly.

It all bigan after I brought home my fancy new pants. I couldn't wear them becaus they were too long. No one eround the house could help me make them shorter. Everyone was too tired. Then, bifor morning, the pants were too short! Someone got up in the night to fix them. This happened agin and then again. Now they are just about perfect for my son.

Spelling Words

1. began
2. again
3. around
4. before
5. away
6. about
7. alive
8. because
9. ahead
10. between
11. behind
12. ago

1. _____   4. _____

2. _____   5. _____

3. _____

Take a Survey Ask two or three friends about what others have done to help them. Take notes.

On a separate sheet of paper, write about how people helped your friends. Use Spelling Words from the list.

Theme 6: **Smart Solutions**   149

Name _____

Antonym Crossword Puzzle

Read each clue. Then choose an antonym from the word bank and fill in the correct boxes on the crossword puzzle. Use a dictionary for help.

Across

2. lost
4. first
6. remember
8. thick

Down

1. slow
3. clean
5. short
6. plain
7. full
9. sad

Name _____

Writing Comparisons

Complete this chart with the correct forms of the adjective.

Adjective	Compare Two Things	Compare More Than Two Things
short	shorter	shortest
loud	1. _____	2. _____
soft	3. _____	4. _____
bold	5. _____	6. _____
quiet	7. _____	8. _____
sharp	9. _____	10. _____

Choose a word from the chart to complete each sentence.

11. The gray fabric is _____ than the red fabric.

12. Big Mama is the _____ ghost.

13. The _____ sound came right after midnight.

14. Aunt Viney is a _____ speaker than Grandma Tiny.

15. Big Mama takes the _____ needle from her sewing kit.

Name _____

Writing the Correct Form

Write the correct form of the adjective in parentheses to complete each sentence.

1. Poppa's new pants are _____ than his old pants. (long)

2. Big Mama is _____ than her sister. (old)

3. Aunt Viney is the _____ sewer of the three ghosts. (fast)

4. The snipping sound is _____ than a whisper. (loud)

5. Grandma Tiny is the _____ of all. (loud)

6. Poppa is _____ than George. (tall)

7. George thinks the second ghost is _____ than the first. (odd)

8. Now Poppa's pants are the _____ pants in the house. (short)

9. George has _____ legs than Poppa. (short)

10. This story is the _____ story I know. (weird)

Name _____

A Good Story, Well Told

Using *good* and *well* Suppose George wrote a letter. Proofread the letter. Check that *good* and *well* are used correctly. Check for spelling errors too. Rewrite the letter below.

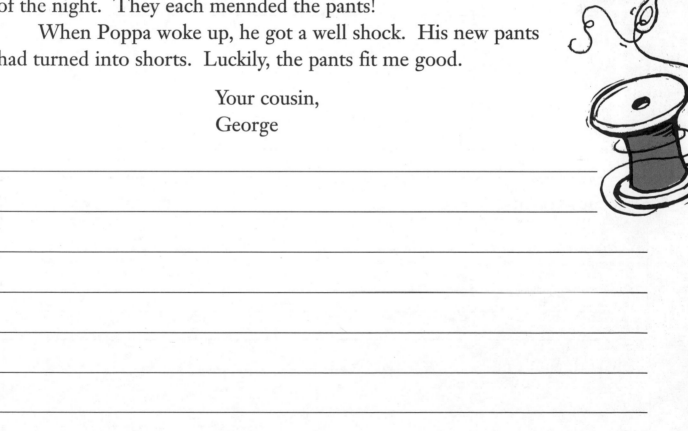

Dear Cousin,

Poppa bought a well new pair of pants last week. But they did not fit him good, so Poppa asked Big Mama, Grandma Tiny, and Aunt Viney to hemm the pants. They said no. Poppa was a little sad, but he is a good man. He didn't complain. Guess what happened next! All three women got up in the middle of the night. They each mennded the pants!

When Poppa woke up, he got a well shock. His new pants had turned into shorts. Luckily, the pants fit me good.

Your cousin,
George

_____

_____

_____

_____

_____

_____

_____

_____

Name _____

Story Map

Use this Story Map to plan a summary of a story you have read recently. Remember to tell who the story is about. Then tell the main things that happened in the story.

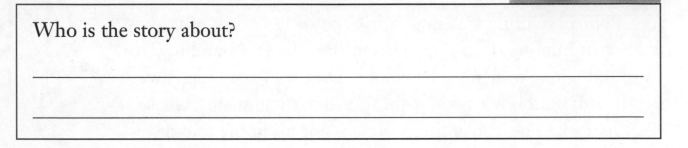

Who is the story about?

_____

_____

Problem

_____

_____

What happens?

_____

_____

How does it end?

_____

_____

Name _____

Paraphrasing

► Paraphrasing is restating something in your own
words, without changing the author's meaning.
► Writers use paraphrasing when they write a
summary or notes for a report.

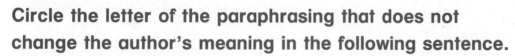

**Circle the letter of the paraphrasing that does not
change the author's meaning in the following sentence.**

"Grandma Tiny's about to bust a gusset making sure
everything's just right."

A. "Grandma Tiny is working hard to make sure everything is
just right."

B. "Grandma Tiny is working so hard that she broke something."

Paraphrase each sentence:

1. Aunt Viney and Big Mama took turns covering my face
with red lipstick.

_____

2. Grandma Tiny, Big Mama, and Aunt Viney usually have a
good long gossip spell when they get together.

_____

_____

3. I stayed balled up under those blankets like an armadillo for
the rest of the night.

_____

4. Grandma Tiny was smiling fit to beat the band.

_____

Name _____

A Rainy-Day Survey!

Write sentences to answer the following questions.

1. Do you think rainy days are **dismal** and **dreary**?
   Why or why not?

   _____

   _____

2. On days when the rain is **ceaseless**, what do you do?

   _____

   _____

3. Do you like the sound of rain **pelting** against your window?

   _____

   _____

4. What do you do when you feel **companionable**?

   _____

   _____

5. What advice would you give to a friend who feels **discouraged**?

   _____

   _____

6. What activity makes you feel **exhausted**?

   _____

   _____

Name _____

Generalizations Chart

Rainy Days	**Older Sisters**
Parents	**Restaurants**

In general, what statement can you make about people's feelings
on rainy days?

_____

_____

Name _____

Ramona's Diary

Suppose Ramona kept a diary. Finish this entry with details from *Ramona Quimby, Age 8*.

Dear Diary,

Sunday afternoon was _____.

Mom and Dad were _____.

Mom kept reminding me to _____.

Then Beezus asked Mom to _____

_____. But Mom and Dad

said no, so Beezus was upset.

Then Dad decided that we should go to the Whopperburger.

He wanted us to _____.

While we were waiting for our seats, _____

_____. Dinner was really tasty

and fun too!

Before the man left, he _____

_____. On the way home, all

of us were _____.

Name _____

Making Cafeteria Food

Read the story below. Then answer the questions on the next page.

Ms. Mallard and Meatloaf

Luis dropped his lunch tray on the table next to his friend Joey and sat down. "Can you believe this? They call this meatloaf!" Luis said. "And they just served it two weeks ago! I can't stand it."

"Then why don't you ask someone why it's always on the menu, Luis?" Joey replied. "All you do is complain."

"You're right. I will." Luis stood up and walked directly back to the serving line where the lunch lady was cleaning up. "Um, Ms. Mallard? Can I ask you something?"

Ms. Mallard turned around. "Ah, yes, of course, Luis. What is it? Enjoying your meatloaf?"

"Not really. That's why I'm here. How come you serve it every two weeks and why does it taste so strange?"

"Well, Luis, schools have rules about the kinds of food we serve," Ms. Mallard responded. "We need to make food that fits in the basic food groups. Meatloaf fits most of them, it's easy to make a lot of, and it doesn't cost much to make. That's why many schools put it on their menus."

"Okay, I get it. But how come it tastes so funny?"

"I can tell you, Luis, that you're not alone on this one. Last summer I went to a national meeting about cafeteria food. Almost everybody I talked to said how much the kids dislike the taste of meatloaf. It probably has something to do with the onions and the peppers in it. Not to mention the dry bread that goes in it. Some people just look at its color and think it can't taste good. That's why. Just try putting ketchup on it."

Name _____

Making Cafeteria Food continued

Answer the following questions based on the story "Ms. Mallard and Meatloaf."

What broad statement can you make about schools and meatloaf?

_____

_____

What details support your generalization?

_____

_____

_____

_____

In general, what can you say about kids and the school meatloaf?

_____

_____

What details support your generalization?

_____

_____

_____

_____

Contraction Puzzler

What did Ramona learn on that rainy Sunday? Solve the puzzle to find out. Write the two words that each contraction is made from. Write only one letter on each line. Then write each numbered letter on the line with the matching number below.

1. we're ____ ____ ____ ____ ____
                    3

2. she's ____ ____ ____ ____
                10   13

3. wasn't ____ ____ ____ ____ ____
                        7

4. you're ____ ____ ____ ____ ____
                            4

5. he'll ____ ____ ____ ____
                1

6. they've ____ ____ ____ ____ ____ ____ ____
                                11   5

7. couldn't ____ ____ ____ ____ ____ ____ ____ ____
            9   14

8. I'm ____ ____ ____
        8   12

9. they'd ____ ____ ____ ____ ____ ____ ____ ____
                    2   15

10. aren't ____ ____ ____ ____ ____ ____
            6

What Ramona learned:

____ ____ ____ ____ ____ ____ ____ ____ ____ ____
 1   2   3   4   5   6   7   8   9   10

f ____ ____ ____ ____ ____
   11   12   13   14   15

Name _____

Contractions

A contraction is a short way of saying or writing two or more words. An apostrophe takes the place of one or more letters.

I am → **I'm**   are not → **aren't**

► The starred words use different patterns.

will not → **won't**   of the clock → **o'clock**

Write each Spelling Word under the heading that tells about it.

Contractions with *not*

Other Contractions

_____   _____

_____   _____

_____   _____

_____   _____

_____   _____

_____

Spelling Spree

Book Titles Write the Spelling Word that best completes each funny book title. Remember to use capital letters.

> **Example:** *No Puzzle I _____ or Wouldn't Solve* by I. M. Smarte Couldn't

1. *The Clock Stopped at One _____* by Minnie T. Hand
2. *_____ You Glad I'm Here?* by Happy A. Ginn
3. *_____ My Brother: A True Story* by N. O. Kidding
4. *The Man Who _____ a Spy* by Minny Kluze

1. _____   3. _____

2. _____   4. _____

Spelling Words

1. I'm
2. he's
3. aren't
4. couldn't
5. won't
6. o'clock*
7. wouldn't
8. weren't
9. she's
10. wasn't
11. I'd
12. shouldn't

Make It Shorter Circle the words below that could be written as contractions. Then write them as contractions on the lines.

5. Mom would not let you do that.

6. You should not even ask her.

7. She is reading the paper.

8. It was not a good idea.

5. _____

6. _____

7. _____

8. _____

Name _____

Proofreading and Writing

Proofreading Suppose Ramona wrote a note.
Circle the five misspelled Spelling Words in the note.
Then write each word correctly.

Sunday, 8 o'clock
Dear Mom and Dad,

    Id like to thank you for taking us to the

Whopperburger. We were'nt having a good day

until then. Even Beezus is happier now, but

she woen't admit it. Aren't you glad the old

man was there? I could'nt believe that he

paid for our meal. I'am glad we're a family.
         Love,
         Ramona

Spelling Words

1. I'm
2. he's
3. aren't
4. couldn't
5. won't*
6. o'clock*
7. wouldn't
8. weren't
9. she's
10. wasn't
11. I'd
12. shouldn't

1. _____   4. _____

2. _____   5. _____

3. _____

Write a Skit Choose a scene to act out from
Ramona Quimby, Age 8, or make up your own
scene with two people from her family.

**Write the words that the characters might say
to each other. Use Spelling Words from the list.**

Name _____

Find the Correct Word

Write the missing word in each sentence. A sample word at the end of each sentence gives a clue about the vowel sound. Find the correct word on the word list and write it in the blank. Then circle the letters in the word that match the vowel sound in the sample word. Look at the spelling table for help.

1. The furnace will _____ the

   whole house. **beast**

2. Lin put on her gloves and _____

   in the snowstorm. **good**

3. The _____ kept my sandwich fresh. **join**

4. The cook placed the pie _____
   into a pan. **though**

5. Birds fly _____ when the weather
   gets cold. **house**

6. What is that lovely _____ coming
   from the kitchen? **went**

Spelling Table

/ă/ bat	/ē/ beast	/ŏ/ pond	/o͝o/ good
/ā/ play	/ĭ/ give	/ō/ though	/o͞o/ house
/â/ care	/ī/ time	/ô/ paw	
/ĕ/ went	/î/ near	/oi/ join	

Name _____

Circling Adverbially

Circle the adverbs in each sentence. Then write the adverbs in the chart below.

1. Ramona watches the rain sadly.

2. Then she looks around in the kitchen.

3. Beezus was crying loudly upstairs.

4. Next, Mrs. Quimby gently scolded Ramona.

5. Nearby, Mr. Quimby read his book silently.

6. Ramona often reads stories to Willa Jean.

7. The pelting rain falls everywhere.

8. "I wanted to bicycle today," she thought sulkily.

9. Finally, Mr. Quimby decided to cheer everyone up.

10. They decided to eat out at Whopperburger.

How	When	Where

Name _____

Choosing Adverbs

Choose an adverb from the box to complete each sentence. Use the clue in parentheses to help you.

Mr. Quimby parked the car and the family walked _____ (where). The customers filled the restaurant _____ (how). Ramona and Beezus quarreled _____ (how). Mrs. Quimby scolded them _____ (how). When they were seated, they ordered _____ (how). Soon the waitress appeared. She carried platters of food _____ (where) of the kitchen.

The Quimbys sat at the table _____ (how). Ramona ate _____ (how). She wished the meal could last forever. She _____ (when) wished for impossible things. Ramona looked _____ (where). She wanted to remember her perfect meal.

Name _____

Expanding Sentences with Adverbs

Add one adverb to each sentence. In the first five sentences, add the adverb in the blank. Use the clues in parentheses to help you. In the other sentences, decide where to add the adverb.

1. Mother talks _____ to Becky. (how)

2. Mother _____ talks to Becky. (when)

3. Becky looks _____ for Fluffy. (where)

4. "I want to sleep over at Mimi's," Susan shouted

   _____. (how)

5. _____ Susan was in tears. (when)

6. Susan slammed her door.

   _____

7. Becky had listened to the quarrel.

   _____

8. She decided to talk to Susan.

   _____

9. "May I come in?" asked Becky.

   _____

10. "Sure," said Susan, "I will only talk to you and our cat."

    _____

Name _____

Planning Your Personal Essay

Use this graphic organizer to help you plan your personal essay. Write your main idea in the top box. Then write two reasons or facts about your idea in the boxes below. Think of details and examples for each reason. Then summarize your main idea in the last box.

My Main Idea:

_____

_____

Reason 1:

_____

_____

Reason 2:

_____

_____

Reason 1 Examples and Details:

_____

_____

_____

Reason 2 Examples and Details:

_____

_____

_____

Summary and restatement of main idea:

_____

_____

Name _____

Telling More with Adverbs

Adverbs can modify verbs. Good writers use adverbs to tell more about an action. They can tell *how* or *when*.

The cat is meowing.

The cat is meowing **loudly**. (tells *how*)

The cat is meowing **now**. (tells *when*)

Adverbs That Tell How		Adverbs That Tell When	
sadly	patiently	always	tomorrow
silently	secretly	finally	now
loudly	quickly	never	daily
slowly		yesterday	

Rewrite each sentence by adding an adverb to tell how or when.

1. The family ate their meals together (when) _____ .

2. Ginger stared (how) _____ out the window.

3. The log in the fireplace snapped (how) _____ .

4. The family waited (how) _____ for a table in the restaurant.

5. The man went to the store (when) _____ .

6. The girl (how) _____ wished for a for a bicycle.

7. He (when) _____ told them about it.

8. The dog ran (how) _____ past the house.

Name _____

Writing a Story

Use what you have learned about taking tests to help you write a story. Take some time to plan what you will write. This practice will help you when you take this kind of test.

In *Pepita Talks Twice*, Pepita decides how to solve her problem. Then she realizes her decision is a bad one. She will miss out on many important things if she sticks to her decision. Write a story about someone who needs to find a smart solution to a problem.

_____

_____

_____

_____

_____

_____

_____

_____

_____

_____

_____

Name _____

Writing a Story continued

Read your story. Check to be sure that

- the beginning introduces the characters, the setting, and the problem
- details bring the story to life
- the events are in an order that makes sense
- the ending tells how the problem works out
- there are few mistakes in capitalization, punctuation, grammar, or spelling

Now pick one way to improve your story. Make your changes below.

_____

_____

_____

_____

_____

_____

_____

_____

_____

_____

_____

Name _____

Spelling Review

Write Spelling Words from the list on this page to answer the questions.

1–8. Which eight words end with *er* or *le*?

1. _____   5. _____

2. _____   6. _____

3. _____   7. _____

4. _____   8. _____

9–14. Which six words begin like the word *asleep*?

9. _____   13. _____

10. _____   14. _____

11. _____

12. _____

15–17. Which three words begin with *be*?

15. _____   17. _____

16. _____

18–25. Which eight words are contractions?

18. _____   22. _____

19. _____   23. _____

20. _____   24. _____

21. _____   25. _____

Spelling Words

1. I'm
2. ago
3. ever
4. around
5. wasn't
6. because
7. little
8. I'd
9. purple
10. again
11. shouldn't
12. November
13. about
14. aren't
15. later
16. apple
17. wouldn't
18. away
19. alive
20. summer
21. before
22. couldn't
23. behind
24. he's
25. able

Name _____

Spelling Spree

Complete the Sentence Fill in the blanks with Spelling Words.

1. My favorite color is _____.

2. Thanksgiving is in _____.

3. Let's have some _____ pie.

4. The mouse ran _____ from the cat.

5. Margo hid _____ a bush.

6. I put on my socks _____ my shoes.

Contraction Action Replace the underlined words with a Spelling Word that is a contraction.

7. I am _____ going to the game with Rico.

8. This is the team I would _____ like to be on.

9. He is _____ the best player on the team.

10. Our uniforms are not _____ very clean now.

11. Last year I could not _____ run as fast as Kara.

12. We all know we should not _____ eat before we swim.

13. Coach would not _____ let us skip practice.

14. The new game was not _____ hard.

Name _____

Proofreading and Writing

Proofreading Circle the five misspelled Spelling Words in this message. Write each word correctly.

Playing soccer is better than hanging arownd. Being on a team is great becuase you make new friends. Two years aggo I was on a team. Now I want to play agin. It is abowt time for tryouts.

1. _____	4. _____
2. _____	5. _____
3. _____	

The Team News Write the Spelling Word that means nearly the opposite of each underlined word or words.

Our team practiced hard this 6. <u>winter</u> _____.

We wanted to be ready 7. <u>after</u> _____ the first game.

We knew if we 8. <u>never</u> _____ wanted to win, we

would have to work. We ended practice 9. <u>earlier</u> _____

every day. We didn't just practice a 10. <u>lot</u> _____. We

have put last year's season 11. <u>in front of</u> _____ us.

Now we hope to be 12. <u>unable</u> _____ to win.

Write an Invitation On a separate sheet of paper, write an invitation to a friend to join a team or club. Use the Spelling Review Words.

Student Handbook

Contents

How to Study a Word

1. LOOK at the word.
► What does the word mean?
► What letters are in the word?
► Name and touch each letter.

2. SAY the word.
► Listen for the consonant sounds.
► Listen for the vowel sounds.

3. THINK about the word.
► How is each sound spelled?
► Close your eyes and picture the word.
► What familiar spelling patterns do you see?
► What other words have the same spelling patterns?

4. WRITE the word.
► Think about the sounds and the letters.
► Form the letters correctly.

5. CHECK the spelling.
► Did you spell the word the same way it is spelled in your word list?
► If you did not spell the word correctly, write the word again.

about	don't	I'd		
again	down	I'll		
almost		I'm	outside	tonight
a lot	enough	into		too
also	every	its	people	two
always	everybody	it's	pretty	
am				until
and	family	January	really	
another	favorite		right	very
anyone	February	knew		
anyway	field	know	said	want
around	finally		Saturday	was
	for	letter	school	Wednesday
beautiful	found	like	some	we're
because	friend	little	something	where
been	from	lose	started	while
before		lying	stopped	who
brought	getting		sure	whole
buy	girl	might	swimming	world
	goes	morning		would
cannot	going	mother	than	wouldn't
can't	guess	myself	that's	write
clothes			their	writing
coming	happily	never	them	
could	have	new	then	you
cousin	haven't	now	there	your
	heard		they	
does	her	off	thought	
didn't	here	one	through	
different	his	other	to	
done	how	our	today	

Seal Surfer

Adding Endings

care– e + ed = car**ed**

save – e + ing = sav**ing**

wrap + p + ed = wrap**ped**

grin + n + ing = grin**ning**

baby – y + ies = bab**ies**

carry – y + ied = carr**ied**

Spelling Words

1. cared
2. babies
3. chopped
4. saving
5. carried
6. fixing
7. hurried
8. joking
9. grinning
10. smiled
11. wrapped
12. parties

Challenge Words

1. moving
2. libraries

My Study List
Add your own
spelling words
on the back. ➡

Animal Habitats
Reading-Writing Workshop

Look for familiar spelling patterns in these words to help you remember their spellings.

Spelling Words

1. girl
2. they
3. want
4. was
5. into
6. who
7. our
8. new
9. would
10. could
11. a lot
12. buy

Challenge Words

1. wouldn't
2. world
3. through
4. while

My Study List
Add your own
spelling words
on the back. ➡

Nights of the Pufflings

The Vowel + /r/ Sounds in *hair*

/âr/ ➡ c**are**, h**air**, b**ear**

Spelling Words

1. hair
2. care
3. chair
4. pair
5. bear
6. where
7. scare
8. air
9. pear
10. bare
11. fair
12. share

Challenge Words

1. flair
2. farewell

My Study List
Add your own
spelling words
on the back. ➡

Name _____

 My Study List

1. _____
2. _____
3. _____
4. _____
5. _____
6. _____
7. _____
8. _____
9. _____
10. _____

Review Words

1. buy
2. could

How to Study a Word

Look at the word.
Say the word.
Think about the word.
Write the word.
Check the spelling.

182

Take-Home Word List

Name _____

 My Study List

1. _____
2. _____
3. _____
4. _____
5. _____
6. _____
7. _____
8. _____
9. _____
10. _____

How to Study a Word

Look at the word.
Say the word.
Think about the word.
Write the word.
Check the spelling.

182

Take-Home Word List

Name _____

My Study List

1. _____
2. _____
3. _____
4. _____
5. _____
6. _____
7. _____
8. _____
9. _____
10. _____

Review Words

1. making
2. stopped

How to Study a Word

Look at the word.
Say the word.
Think about the word.
Write the word.
Check the spelling.

182

Across the Wide Dark Sea

The Vowel Sounds in _tooth_ and _cook_

/ōō/ ➡ t**oo**th, ch**ew**

/ŏŏ/ ➡ c**oo**k

Spelling Words

1. tooth
2. chew
3. grew
4. cook
5. shoe
6. blue
7. boot
8. flew
9. shook
10. balloon
11. drew
12. spoon

Challenge Words

1. loose
2. brook

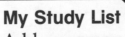

My Study List
Add your own spelling words on the back. ➡

Animal Habitats

Spelling Review

Spelling Words

1. pair
2. unhurt
3. grinning
4. air
5. smiled
6. sadly
7. care
8. retell
9. babies
10. bear
11. unlike
12. cared
13. scare
14. hopeful
15. parties
16. pear
17. remake
18. chopped
19. bare
20. unhappy
21. joking
22. chair
23. friendly
24. carried
25. helper

See the back for Challenge Words

My Study List
Add your own spelling words on the back. ➡

Two Days in May

Prefixes and Suffixes

re + make = **re**make

un + happy = **un**happy

care + **ful** = care**ful**

friend + **ly** = friend**ly**

help + **er** = help**er**

Spelling Words

1. helper
2. unfair
3. friendly
4. unhappy
5. remake
6. careful
7. hopeful
8. unlike
9. retell
10. sadly
11. farmer
12. unhurt

Challenge Words

1. unimportant
2. silently

My Study List
Add your own spelling words on the back. ➡

Name _____

 My Study List

1. _____
2. _____
3. _____
4. _____
5. _____
6. _____
7. _____
8. _____
9. _____
10. _____

Review Words

1. have
2. said

How to Study a Word

Look at the word.
Say the word.
Think about the word.
Write the word.
Check the spelling.

Name _____

 My Study List

1. _____
2. _____
3. _____
4. _____
5. _____
6. _____
7. _____
8. _____
9. _____
10. _____

Challenge Words

1. farewell
2. flair
3. moving
4. libraries
5. silently

How to Study a Word

Look at the word.
Say the word.
Think about the word.
Write the word.
Check the spelling.

Name _____

 My Study List

1. _____
2. _____
3. _____
4. _____
5. _____
6. _____
7. _____
8. _____
9. _____
10. _____

Review Words

1. good
2. soon

How to Study a Word

Look at the word.
Say the word.
Think about the word.
Write the word.
Check the spelling.

Trapped by the Ice!

The VCCV Pattern

VC | CV

Mon | day

sud | den

Spelling Words

1. Monday
2. sudden
3. until
4. forget
5. happen
6. follow
7. dollar
8. window
9. hello
10. market
11. pretty
12. order

Challenge Words

1. stubborn
2. expect

My Study List
Add your own spelling words on the back. ➡

Yunmi and Halmoni's Trip

The Vowel Sound in *bought*

/ô/ ➡ b**ough**t, c**augh**t

Spelling Words

1. caught
2. thought
3. bought
4. laugh
5. through
6. enough
7. fought
8. daughter
9. taught
10. brought
11. ought
12. cough

Challenge Words

1. sought
2. granddaughter

My Study List
Add your own spelling words on the back. ➡

Voyagers Reading-Writing Workshop

Look for familiar spelling patterns in these words to help you remember their spellings.

Spelling Words

1. down
2. how
3. its
4. coming
5. stopped
6. started
7. wrote
8. swimming
9. from
10. write
11. writing
12. brought

Challenge Words

1. favorite
2. sure
3. clothes
4. heard

My Study List
Add your own spelling words on the back. ➡

Name _____

 **My Study List**

1. _____
2. _____
3. _____
4. _____
5. _____
6. _____
7. _____
8. _____
9. _____
10. _____

How to Study a Word

Look at the word.
Say the word.
Think about the word.
Write the word.
Check the spelling.

Name _____

 My Study List

1. _____
2. _____
3. _____
4. _____
5. _____
6. _____
7. _____
8. _____
9. _____
10. _____

Review Words

1. teeth
2. was

How to Study a Word

Look at the word.
Say the word.
Think about the word.
Write the word.
Check the spelling.

Name _____

 My Study List

1. _____
2. _____
3. _____
4. _____
5. _____
6. _____
7. _____
8. _____
9. _____
10. _____

Review Words

1. after
2. funny

How to Study a Word

Look at the word.
Say the word.
Think about the word.
Write the word.
Check the spelling.

Smart Solutions

Reading-Writing Workshop

Look for familiar spelling patterns in these words to help you remember their spellings.

Spelling Words

1. his
2. I'd
3. I'm
4. that's
5. didn't
6. don't
7. know
8. outside
9. been
10. we're
11. anyone
12. anyway

Challenge Words

1. lose
2. finally
3. different
4. happily

My Study List
Add your own spelling words on the back. ➡

Pepita Talks Twice

Words That End with _er_ or _le_

/ər/ ➡ summ**er**

/əl/ ➡ litt**le**

Spelling Words

1. summer
2. winter
3. little
4. October
5. travel
6. color
7. apple
8. able
9. November
10. ever
11. later
12. purple

Challenge Words

1. thermometer
2. mumble

My Study List
Add your own spelling words on the back. ➡

Voyagers

Spelling Review

Spelling Words

1. grew
2. daughter
3. until
4. cook
5. ought
6. forget
7. balloon
8. caught
9. dollar
10. boot
11. window
12. taught
13. flew
14. brought
15. hello
16. tooth
17. Monday
18. pretty
19. chew
20. sudden
21. order
22. spoon
23. thought
24. happen
25. bought

See the back for Challenge Words

My Study List
Add your own spelling words on the back. ➡

Take-Home Word List

Take-Home Word List

Name _____

 **My Study List**

1. _____
2. _____
3. _____
4. _____
5. _____
6. _____
7. _____
8. _____
9. _____
10. _____

Name _____

 My Study List

1. _____
2. _____
3. _____
4. _____
5. _____
6. _____
7. _____
8. _____
9. _____
10. _____

Name _____

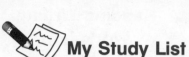 **My Study List**

1. _____
2. _____
3. _____
4. _____
5. _____
6. _____
7. _____
8. _____
9. _____
10. _____

Challenge Words

1. brook
2. expect
3. loose
4. stubborn
5. granddaughter

Review Words

1. flower
2. people

How to Study a Word

Look at the word.
Say the word.
Think about the word.
Write the word.
Check the spelling.

How to Study a Word

Look at the word.
Say the word.
Think about the word.
Write the word.
Check the spelling.

How to Study a Word

Look at the word.
Say the word.
Think about the word.
Write the word.
Check the spelling.

Smart Solutions
Spelling Review
Spelling Words

1. little
2. again
3. summer
4. alive
5. purple
6. around
7. I'm
8. able
9. wouldn't
10. ago
11. ever
12. before
13. aren't
14. I'd
15. because
16. wouldn't
17. away
18. couldn't
19. November
20. shouldn't
21. apple
22. about
23. behind
24. wasn't
25. later

See the back for Challenge Words

My Study List
Add your own spelling words on the back.➡

189

Ramona Quimby, Age 8

Contractions
A **contraction** is a short way of writing two or more words. An apostrophe replaces any dropped letters.

Spelling Words

1. I'm
2. he's
3. aren't
4. couldn't
5. won't
6. o'clock
7. wouldn't
8. weren't
9. she's
10. wasn't
11. I'd
12. shouldn't

Challenge Words
1. let's
2. who's

My Study List
Add your own spelling words on the back.➡

189

Poppa's New Pants

Words That Begin with *a* or *be*

/ə/ ➡ **a**gain
/bĭ/ ➡ **be**fore

Spelling Words

1. began
2. again
3. around
4. before
5. away
6. about
7. alive
8. because
9. ahead
10. between
11. behind
12. ago

Challenge Words
1. awhile
2. beyond

My Study List
Add your own spelling words on the back.➡

189

Name _____

 My Study List

1. _____
2. _____
3. _____
4. _____
5. _____
6. _____
7. _____
8. _____
9. _____
10. _____

Review Words

1. they
2. want

How to Study a Word

Look at the word.
Say the word.
Think about the word.
Write the word.
Check the spelling.

Name _____

My Study List

1. _____
2. _____
3. _____
4. _____
5. _____
6. _____
7. _____
8. _____
9. _____
10. _____

Review Words

1. can't
2. isn't

How to Study a Word

Look at the word.
Say the word.
Think about the word.
Write the word.
Check the spelling.

Name _____

My Study List

1. _____
2. _____
3. _____
4. _____
5. _____
6. _____
7. _____
8. _____
9. _____
10. _____

Challenge Words

1. mumble
2. let's
3. awhile
4. who's
5. thermometer

How to Study a Word

Look at the word.
Say the word.
Think about the word.
Write the word.
Check the spelling.

Problem Words

Words	Rules	Examples
are our	*Are* is a verb. *Our* is a possessive pronoun.	<u>Are</u> these gloves yours? This is <u>our</u> car.
doesn't don't	Use *doesn't* with singular nouns, *he*, *she*, and *it*. Use *don't* with plural nouns, *I*, *you*, *we*, and *they*.	Dad <u>doesn't</u> swim. We <u>don't</u> swim.
good well	Use the adjective *good* to describe nouns. Use the adverb *well* to describe verbs.	The weather looks <u>good</u>. She sings <u>well</u>.
its it's	*Its* is a possessive pronoun. *It's* means "*it is*" (contraction).	The dog wagged <u>its</u> tail. <u>It's</u> cold today.
let leave	*Let* means "to allow." *Leave* means "to go away from" or "to let stay."	Please <u>let</u> me go swimming. I will <u>leave</u> soon. <u>Leave</u> it on my desk.
set sit	*Set* means "to put." *Sit* means "to rest or stay in one place."	<u>Set</u> the vase on the table. Please <u>sit</u> in this chair.
their there they're	*Their* means "belonging to them." *There* means "at or in that place." *They're* means "*they are*" (contraction).	<u>Their</u> coats are on the bed. Is Carlos <u>there</u>? <u>They're</u> going to the store.
two to too	*Two* is a number. *To* means "toward." *Too* means "also" or "more than enough."	I bought <u>two</u> shirts. A cat ran <u>to</u> the tree. Can we go <u>too</u>? I ate <u>too</u> many peas.
your you're	*Your* is a possessive pronoun. *You're* means "*you are*" (contraction).	Are these <u>your</u> glasses? <u>You're</u> late again!

Read each question below. Then check your paper. Correct any mistakes you find. After you have corrected them, put a check mark in the box next to the question.

☐ 1. Did I indent each paragraph?

☐ 2. Does each sentence tell one complete thought?

☐ 3. Did I end each sentence with the correct mark?

☐ 4. Did I begin each sentence with a capital letter?

☐ 5. Did I use capital letters correctly in other places?

☐ 6. Did I use commas correctly?

☐ 7. Did I spell all the words the right way?

Are there other problem areas you should watch for? Make your own proofreading checklist.

☐ _____

☐ _____

☐ _____

☐ _____

☐ _____

☐ _____

☐ _____

☐ _____

Mark	Explanation	Examples
¶	Begin a new paragraph. Indent the paragraph.	¶We went to an air show last Saturday. Eight jets flew across the sky in the shape of V's, X's, and diamonds.
∧	Add letters, words, or sentences.	The leaves were red ∧and orange.
℘	Take out words, sentences, and punctuation marks. Correct spelling.	The sky is bright ~~blew.~~ blue. Huge clouds, move quickly.
/	Change a capital letter to a small letter.	The /Fireflies blinked in the dark.
≡	Change a small letter to a capital letter.	New York c̲i̲t̲y̲ is exciting.